Jacques Lacan and Education

Jacques Lacan and Education

A Critical Introduction

Donyell L. Roseboro
University of North Carolina at Wilmington

SENSE PUBLISHERS
ROTTERDAM / TAIPEI

A C.I.P. record for this book is available from the Library of Congress.

ISBN: 978-90-8790-423-4 (paperback)
ISBN: 978-90-8790-424-1 (hardback)
ISBN: 978-90-8790-425-8 (e-book)

Published by: Sense Publishers,
P.O. Box 21858, 3001 AW
Rotterdam, The Netherlands

Printed on acid-free paper

For my father, Donald Walter Phillips, who lives defiantly and truthfully.
With courage, I have faced Lacan and I have learned.

For my mother, Flora Riddick Phillips, who models grace and conviction.
With fortitude, I will always be a teacher.

TABLE OF CONTENTS

ACKNOWLEDGEMENTS

To Joe Kincheloe for illuminating moments of clarity in the vast ambiguity of Lacan.

To Richard Allen for his formatting of the manuscript.

To Lindsay Dunham for her careful proofreading. Any errors which remain are entirely my own.

To my mom, for listening and engaging in dialogue with me about Lacan.

To my husband, Bratis D. Roseboro, for making life possible while reading and writing Lacan.

To my girls, Ciera Joi and Maya Jasmin, for making life so wonderful despite Lacan.

CHAPTER 1

LACAN AS PSYCHOANLAYST AND TEACHER

INTRODUCTION

As with any work, I find it necessary to situate myself before beginning. I am an educational philosopher, a critical pedagogue who specializes in cultural studies. I am not a psychoanalyst. When I first encountered Lacan, it was as a doctoral student and the class was one in feminist theory. While this may seem like a strange place to have encountered Lacan (a man whom some feminists love to hate); it was a unique place, one that piqued my interest. And so, I continued reading only to discover that his writing was, at best, slippery, and, at worst, maddening. My competitiveness would not let him undo me and, eventually, I began to see Lacan's writings as mysteries with alternate endings. For me, this has been and remains a learning process, one in which I rely upon the deep body of knowledge already produced by psychoanalytic students of Lacan.

Because Lacan considered himself a Freudian, he extensively studied Freud's topography (mapping) of the ego (rational self), id (pleasure seeking unconscious drive) and the superego (moral/ethical preconscious drive). Lacan was also, however, a student of structural linguistics and wed his psychoanalytic theory with language theory. Reality, for Lacan, existed within language. To understand Lacan then is to accept that we are who we are because of language and, because language has form and structure, we are inherently bound to/by that structure. With his psychoanalytic and linguistic theories, Lacan captured human relations in linguistic space, at the intersection of thought, speech, and the written word.

It is here that I entered Lacanian theory with interest. As an educator committed to the creation of democratic classroom spaces, spaces in which students are engaged in personally meaningful learning experiences, I craved a way to bridge the divide between the personally meaningful and the intellectual. Though I never see the two as mutually exclusive, I have endured countless accountability measures and standardized testing procedures which embrace only the intellectual and ignore the emotional or affective. With Lacan's analysis of identity and language, I found a new educative space, one which hinges in the theoretical nexus between psychoanalysis, structural linguistics, and critical pedagogy. In this space, I explore the connections between identity, language, and education.

As a critical pedagogue, I challenge the presumption that what we do in schools is, in fact education. Any number of other terms might apply — compulsory attending or banking — but it is not educating in the spirit of the term. Educating can not be reduced to proficiency scores on standardized tests, tests which measure one's ability to regurgitate or guess effectively rather than one's ability to critically problem solve. In a more specific sense, I believe that education should be democratic in process and content. How and what we learn should connect to the founding principles of American government—life, liberty, and the pursuit of happiness. Educating should be about creating spaces in which children learn to live organic and productive lives. It should be about creating spaces in which children learn to define freedom and learn to practice living as free and conscientious members of a larger community. And, finally, it should be about creating spaces in which children learn happiness in the spiritual and unselfish sense of the word, a happiness that reflects and speaks to their learning to live as integrated human beings.

This does not mean that I believe democratic education is "content free," that somehow children need not learn to read, write, or multiply. Rather, I believe and hope that democratic education is intrinsically integrated; that whatever is studied (whether that is science, music, drama, art, or history) always connects to children's lived experiences in some way. Equally important, my vision of democratic education demands that teachers engage with students as learning professionals, respectful of the knowledge students bring and cognizant of teaching as an intrinsic and extrinsic process. It is a process that requires us, as educators (or future educators) to examine ourselves as we also examine our students and the social and cultural environments in which we live.

In this context, I use Lacan's theories as a springboard for a different educational discourse, one that forces us to assess inward rather than outward. To move beyond the linear nature of schools, a context exacerbated by developmental psychologists like Piaget and Erikson who theorized that we can understand children's development in stages, I argue that Lacan's theories allow us to holistically educate — to teach cognizant of the relationship between interior and exterior spaces, between the unspoken and the heard.

Using this context, I have organized this book purposefully with specific emphasis on Lacan's work as a teacher and less focus on the evolution of his theories. Since I am foregrounding the concepts of identity, language, and democratic education, I frame the chapters around the Lacanian theories that specifically relate to those subjects. I must caution here that I do this because this is an introductory level text and because my emphasis is on Lacan's theoretical relationship to education. Any psychoanalyst who is a sincere student of Lacan would (with good reason) argue that, to truly engage with Lacan, one would need to study the evolution of his theoretical thought from the beginning of his career until then end because Lacan, like most theorists, spent his entire life developing, revising, and reclaiming certain ideas. For this reason, there are few theoretical points that remain unchanged throughout his career. It is precisely this instability which makes Lacan so compelling as an educator — he spends his entire life learning *and* teaching.

In chapter one, I situate Lacan historically and theoretically. His identity theories, understood in conjunction with nationalist and imperialist tendencies which pervaded Europe during the 1930's and 1940's as well as the global social unrest of the 1960's, provide the basis for my discussion of the self in relation, the convergence or divergence of self and group identities. Lacan's historical location socializes his theory; it gives us a context for the development of his theories of the self and language. Also in this chapter, I outline Lacan's Freudian roots and his work (some might say escapades) as a clinical practitioner. In chapter two, I introduce Lacan's concept of the mirror stage. Simply put, Lacan argued that infants would, at some point between the ages of six and eighteen months, come to recognize themselves in the mirror (or in reflection)[1]; they would realize that the baby in the mirror is not some other child. I will explore this concept of identity formation with attention to the ways in which mirroring and reflexivity continually shape the self identities we create. Chapter 3 discusses Lacan's interpretation of language and his application of it in his teaching and writing. In this chapter, I work with Lacan's idea that language, with its inconsistency and fallibility, shapes our existence. Here I am equally concerned with Lacan's theorizing about language and his use of it. In his theory, he connects with structuralism, but in his speaking and writing, he persistently pushes the limits of language struggling to find new discursive spaces. Here, I will consider Lacan's attempts to find new language a metaphor for the struggles faced by teachers and students in trying to find common discourse, a discourse that mediates between the worlds of home and school.

Finally, in Chapters four, five, and six I will examine Lacan as a clinical practitioner within postmodern, post-structural, and post-formal theories. All of these theories speak to identity formation and subjectivity; they re-conceptualize the self/other nexus and deconstruct the notion that the self is stable and singular. These theories, considered in parallel to Lacan, stimulate further questioning of intersections between group and self identities. Chapter five thus negotiates the influence of postmodern, post-structural, and post-formal theories on education. Chapter six ends with a negotiation of several critical questions. Can the invented be the inventor? If so, how must we redefine identity in that context? What are the implications for democratic public education? How might a paradigm shift in identity definition and/or developmental theory possibly reshape pedagogy? How might such a shift reframe the ways we do and think curriculum? And, how might such a shift uncover different language, a discourse that embraces children as competent and whole human beings rather than deficient and disconnected parts?

LACAN'S HISTORICAL CONTEXT

In 1901, Alfred Lacan and Emilie Baudry gave birth to their first child, Jacques-Marie Emile Lacan. It was the turn of the century in France, a time when the nation's Catholic constituency pushed for government to reflect and represent that Catholic heritage. In the midst of this fervour, anti-semitism rose and Jewish citizens found themselves at the center of a national debate which pitted Catholics against Jews. One case, in particular, reflected the sentiment of the era—the Dreyfus affair. When, in 1894, Alfred Dreyfus, a Jewish captain in the French army was charged with providing military information to Germany, conflict erupted between representatives of the French republic, top level military officers and Catholic officials. Despite finding evidence to prove Dreyfus' innocence, the military refused to release Dreyfus. By 1899, the president of France pardoned Dreyfus but he could not return to Paris until 1906. By this time (and after witnessing the involvement of Catholic priests in the attacks against Dreyfus), the government had passed legislation which called for the separation of church and state. Into this highly charged political climate Lacan entered the world. His family, a prosperous Roman Catholic merchant family, established themselves in the food business by selling and trading in rum, brandy, and coffee. By 1907, Lacan's parents had given birth to three more children, Raymond (who lived for just two years), Madeleine, and Marc-Marie. Between 1907 and 1919, Lacan had attended school at the Collège Stanislas and he had begun to study medicine.

By 1927 Lacan was in clinical training for psychiatry and within the next three years, he had written six neurological studies based on psychiatric cases. He continued his clinical training in other venues, including the Paris Police Special Infirmary for the Insane and the Hospital Henri Rouselle. For the next ten years, until 1937, Lacan's career began to blossom as he continued writing and publishing his work. He did not go without his own share of troubles, however; in 1936, when he presented a paper on the mirror stage, he left abruptly after being interrupted by an audience member and, in 1938, he spent considerable time re-writing an article because editors complained that it was too obscure. In his personal life, Lacan faced additional troubles. After marrying Marie-Louise Blondin in 1934 and having three children with her, Lacan had another child with Sylvia Maklès-Bataille. He and Marie-Louise divorced soon afterwards and the events of World War II soon overshadowed his personal trials.

During the war, the Société psychoanalytique de Paris ceased all official activity and Lacan traveled to Britain for a little over a month. During his time in Britain, he studied with British psychiatrists and evaluated their wartime psychiatric practice. Over the next forty years, Lacan would continue his clinical practice, introducing psychoanalytic sessions of variable length (a practice that was condemned by the Société psychoanalytique de Paris). During his lifetime, he met and developed friendships with a variety of great thinkers including the Surrealist theorist/writer André Breton, the artists Salvador Dalí, and Pablo Picasso, the existentialist Jean-Paul Satre, the phenomenologist Maurice Merleau-Ponty, anthropologist Claude Lévi-Strauss, psychoanalyst Carl Jung, French Communist philosopher Louis Althusser, and German philosopher Martin Heidegger. When he died on September 9 at the age of 81, Lacan had inspired, provoked, and challenged thousands of people who had attended his public seminars at St. Anne's in Paris or students who attended one of his seminars at the Ecole normale supércure, rue d'Ulm or at the law faculty at the place du Panthéon.

He had witnessed the ravaging of his country in two world wars, the manipulation of his government by Germans in World War II, the resistance movement led by Charles de Gaulle during that same war, student strikes in the late 1960's, and the coalescence of an international feminist movement in the early 1970's. His presence in the international arena had even personally touched some American students in 1966 when he visited six universities including Harvard, MIT, and Columbia and in 1975 when he visited Yale, Columbia, and MIT. He was a teacher who believed that history shaped psychoanalysis. Lacanian psychoanalyst and translator Bruce Fink (2004) says, "According to Lacan, the relationship between history and psychoanalysis is a very intimate one indeed, psychoanalysis having taken as its first task to fill the gaps in the subject's history and to probe the unusual temporality in the subject's history—the past being what is repressed" (p. 42). If then the subject's history is repressed, then it represents part of the unconscious (the id) and operates like a text that the psychoanalyst and analysand (psychiatric patient or subject) must learn to read.

For as much as Lacan was a practicing psychoanalyst, he also believed that studying the history of psychoanalysis would reveal some truth about the nature of human existence. Since Lacan is critical of psychoanalysts who claimed psychoanalysis could be entirely curative, he hoped that evaluating the history of psychoanalysis would lead him towards some greater understanding of how to change the direction of the field itself. He wanted to examine the idea "that the evolution and transformations of analytic experience teach us about the very nature of this experience insofar as it is also a human experience that is hidden from itself" (Seminar I, 32/24). His theoretical connection between the field of psychoanalysis and history becomes even more important as we consider its implications for social history or, as Lacan himself would frame it, the social unconscious. Lacan's theory would suggest that, if we perceive of history as part of the unconscious, then we psychologically repress that history and that the psychoanalytic process will help us learn to read and engage with those repressed memories.

Lacan sought, through his study of ego psychology and object relations, to traverse a critical impasse in the history of psychoanalysis. Many psychoanalytic theorists of the late 1930's and early 1940's, most notably Anna Freud (daughter of Freud), had studied in great detail Freud's initial explanation of ego psychology. Freud had argued that the ego did not come into being as separate from the id (unconscious). Some of these psychoanalytic theorists chose to ignore Freud's initial characterization of the ego as a part of the unconscious. They took Anna Freud's emphasis of the ego as proof positive that the ego was worthy of separation, worthy of study as a distinct entity. These theorists claimed that their discarding of Freud's initial explanation was simply a synchronization of his concepts but, in doing so, they ignored the importance of analyzing the historical development of Freud's rationale. In fact, Lacan took them to task for failing to appreciate the tension between Freud's claim that the ego could control a subject's actions while it also stemmed from the unconscious (Fink, 2004).

Because Lacan valued the historical evolution of psychoanalytic theory, he brought back Freud's idea that the ego's birthplace is in the unconscious. He studied the ego in the unconscious or, in his words, the "subject of the unconscious." With this restoration/repositioning of the subject to the unconscious, Lacan effectively de-centered the ego. His revitalization of the contradictions in Freud's theory (namely, that the ego controlled actions but that the ego was not, at least initially, distinct from the unconscious—the subject of the unconscious controls actions), brought forth a litany of psychoanalytic debate. Fink (2004) argues that, both Lacan and the Anna Freudian group (those who ignored Freud's claim that the ego was a part of the unconscious), had valid interpretations of Freud's theory; the theory was complicated and contradictory. Fink illuminates for us the importance of Lacan re-reading of Freud to the evolution of psychoanalytic thought. Fink says,

> What we can say is that, historically speaking, Hartman's reading was sterile and unproductive. It led to very little in the way of a renewal of research and theorization, whereas Lacan's led to a huge increase in both (like a good interpretation in the analytic setting, it generated a lot of new material). We can also say that Lacan's approach gave a considerable impetus to practice (p. 45).

In contrast, theorists like Heinz Hartman used Freud to perpetuate developmental psychology, a concept rooted in the belief that children moved through cognitive stages. Lacan not only disputed developmental psychology, he also claimed that it was antithetical to the spirit of psychoanalysis. Psychoanalysis could potentially illuminate much more complicated, contextualized, relational human development; to reduce it to simplistic linear stages would divorce psychoanalysis from its infinite possibility as a method of reading/re-reading the subject.

LACAN AND PHILOSPHY

Lacan studied Nietzsche, Kierkegaard, Marx, Hegel, Kant, Descartes, Aristotle, Plato, Pascal, Newton, Hegel, and numerous others. His interest in and engagement with philosophy spanned different philosophical traditions and disciplines from science to humanities to mathematics and linguistics. Lacan uses philosophy as a point of departure and contention, one in which he elaborates on the nature of truth and reality, knowledge and ethics. In his seminar, "Beyond the Reality Principle," he went so far as to say, "For while I consider it legitimate to privilege the historical method in studying facts of consciousness, I do not use it as a pretext to elude the intrinsic critique that questions their value" (Écrits, 74). He went on to conclude that, if we traced the historical evolution of psychology, we would discover that many psychoanalysts claiming to have some new interpretation were really borrowing from philosophy (Écrits, 74). And, in this borrowing, many compared psychology to science and claimed to have arrived at some new truth or some new explanation of reality. Lacan, in fact, critiqued the prior association of psychology with exact science because, as he said, "truth in its specific value remains foreign to science: science can be proud of its alliances with truth; it can adopt the phenomenon and value of truth as its object; but it cannot in any way identify truth as its own end" (Écrits, 79).

For Lacan, truth was a matter of representation. It was a matter of what could be captured by language. The question of language was one that, according to Lacan, prevented science from claiming "the search for truth" as its main goal. To illustrate his point, Lacan uses an example,

> Can we say that scientists wonder if the rainbow is *true*? All that matters to them is that this phenomenon is communicable in some language (the condition of the *intellectual order*), that it be reportable in some form (the

> condition of the *experimental order*), and that it be possible to insert into the chain of symbolic identifications with which their science unifies the diversity of its own object (the condition of the *rational order*) (Écrits, 79).

What is communicable through language is, perhaps, our best representation of what is true. Lacan's combination of historical method, psychoanalytic inquiry, and structural linguistics would come together to push the question of truth even further. His re-reading of Freud would lead him to question the relationship between truth, the unconscious, and language.

Lacan's interest in the unconscious, or the subject of the unconscious, leads him to suggest that there is a part of the unconscious that will remain forever unknown despite the best efforts of psychoanalysis. The unconscious represents that which cannot be directly explained through language. Unconscious thought may enter the world through language, but it does so in indirect, convoluted ways. With the help of psychoanalysis, a subject may begin to interpret unconscious desires that manifest themselves through speech, action, or dreams in various ways, but even psychoanalysis cannot explain/define the unconscious in precise ways. In fact, Lacan specifically says,

> There is often a passage in even the most thoroughly interpreted dream which has to be left obscure; this is because we become aware during the work of interpretation that at that point there is a tangle of dream-thoughts which cannot be unraveled and which moreover adds nothing to our knowledge of the content of the dream. This is the dream's naval, the spot where it reaches down into the unknown (SE 5, p. 525/Shepherdson, 2003, p. 117).

Because Lacan wed his theory to structural linguistics, he believed that representation, reality, what is known, is tied to language. Psychoanalysis, as a method of interpretation dependent upon the spoken word, was bound by language. And because language had/has limits, psychoanalysts would always find themselves limited in their ability to interpret the unconscious.

For Lacan, there were three realms of knowing — the real, the symbolic, or the imaginary orders. Psychoanalysts study the symbolic order, that which is represented by discourse. The real is that part of the universe that we cannot capture in/through language. And the imaginary represents a Hegelian intersubjectivity, an understanding of one's self. Lacan visually represents the relationship between the real, the imaginary and the symbolic with a triangle. Each side of the triangle is connected by directional arrows with arrows pointing from the real to the imaginary to the symbolic to the real. The real is located in the bottom right corner, the imaginary is the top and the symbolic is located in the lower left corner. The right side of the triangle represents reality, the left side represents truth, and the bottom side represents semblance (83). The imaginary is the locus of the ego and, as such, a mediator between the symbolic and the real. Lacan believes that there will always be an unknown part of the unconscious, a part that escapes definition in language. His theories reflect a constant engagement with the complexity and obscurity of the unconscious.

With his emphasis on the unconscious and his return to Freudian psychology, Lacan called attention to the ego (self). But for Lacan, the juxtaposition of the ego with the unconscious makes the ego much less stable — it is a site of murkiness rather than a site of coherence. Lacan called into question our ability to know ourselves. He does not follow the Cartesian logic "I think, therefore I am," because, for Lacan, much of what we think is beyond our ability to translate into language. Even further, Lacan did not believe that thought presupposed being. Rather, he argued that "being," as a subject defined by language, determined one's thought. In this case, the subject is not merely an "I" or the ego. It is the "speaking being" that is the subject. Through the symbolic order of language, the subject coalesces and comes forth (Écrits & Campbell, 2004).

For this reason, the Lacanian subject is not a material, physical entity. It represents, instead, a relationship between words or, to be more specific, a relationship between the meanings of words (a concept I will explore later, in chapter 4). The subject does not merely "know" her/himself. Rather, s/he represents what is known through language. S/he is created by the unconscious and language, two factors that set limits *and* offer possibilities. Here again, we must return to Lacan as historical psychoanalytic practitioner. If bound by language and if language is constituted in time and in relationship, then the subject represents an intersection of the past and the future. Thus, the Lacanian subject is temporal, connected in complex ways to the realm of the Imaginary (the self), the Real (the unspeakable), and the Symbolic (language).

If we return to the question of "what is real" and "what is true?", then we must translate Lacan's theory of the subject into a question of epistemology and cognition. As Campbell (2004) says, "For Lacan, the question 'how do I know?' entails another question: 'who am I?'" (p. 31). How and when we learn to frame these questions becomes a critical point in the development of the ego or, in other words, in our developing self awareness. This developing self awareness entices Lacan and marks the significance of psychoanalytic practice. Through the psychoanalytic process, Lacan envisions the development of the knowing subject, a subject capable of recognizing its unconscious desires (even if these desires cannot be translated initially) and temporality; the psychoanalytic process is a dialectic one in which the analysand (person being analyzed) comes to understand her/himself as incomplete. To know one's self is to recognize one's mobility in language — if we are defined by and within language, then we are subject to the many detours of language.

LACAN AS TEACHER/PERFORMER

To re-read Lacan with the discourse of democratic education demands that we attune ourselves to his pedagogy. How did he teach? How do his writings represent his theoretical and clinical processes as well as his style? It is clear from Lacan's life and work that he preferred oratory. His constant travails with writing, his reluctance to publish his work, and his belief in the limits of language combined to make him more than a little suspicious of the written word. In writing he felt confined and worried that people would read his theories as static rather than malleable. Fink (2004) best summarizes Lacan's privileging of his teaching over his writing. He says,

> But writing, even this kind of writing, has its dangers too: The reader might be inclined to take a given text as a system or a doctrine and pick it apart, or 'deconstruct' it…This is dangerous to Lacan for at least two reasons: 1) His work is declarative rather than demonstrative, and the reader is hard pressed to find an argument in it to sustain any one particular claim…2) He has a tendency to want to avoid being pinned down to any one particular formulation of things…(65).

He valued the interactive space of his seminars but this does not mean that he necessarily valued interruption or contention. In his speaking and writing, he sought to steer the listener's/reader's thoughts into a particular direction. In 1936, when he was speaking at the Marienbad Congress, Ernest Jones (then president of the London Psycho-analytic society and moderator of the Congress proceedings) interrupted Lacan's talk as he was about ten minutes into his speech. After the interruption, Lacan left abruptly and later refused to submit his paper for inclusion in the conference proceedings (Écrits, 184). He then comments in "The instance of the letter in the unconscious" that "writing is in fact distinguished by a prevalence of the *text* in the sense that we will see this factor of discourse take on here—which allows for the kind of tightening up that must, to my taste, leave the reader no other way out than the way in, which I prefer to be difficult" (Écrits, 493). Lacan, in his writing, exercised more control over the evolution of his theories. For this reason, he spent considerable time re-working his seminars, refining and reframing the language, not necessarily to make it more precise, but to make it more resistant to precision (Fink, 2004).

In other ways, Lacan wrote to purposefully elude explanation. His interest in Surrealism, poetry, languages, and mathematics led him to use his writing as an exploration in the presentation of reality. He would interchange terms, intersperse his French with Latin and German, and frame his theoretical expositions as rhythmic prose. In his 1955/56 essay, "The Freudian Thing," Lacan presents Truth as a speaking "I," one that delivers an extensive speech. Rabaté (2003) characterizes Lacan's style as dense and maintains that his critics caricatured him as a "hamming buffoon" even as they simultaneously admired his "personal openness, professional rigor, and availability" (p. 5). Rabaté goes on to say that Lacan's critics wondered if Lacan was "a frustrated poet, a post-Heideggarian thinker progressing by opaque epigrams, a psychoanalyst wishing to revolutionize a whole field of knowledge, or just a charlatan?" (p. 5). I believe that Lacan embraced the idea of performativity in teaching, that he looked for ways to teach that were radically different, and that, ultimately, his more abstract performances represented his challenge to students. He hoped that his performances would create definitive interest and engagement in his seminars.

Lacan's allegiance to his students and disdain for higher level administrators comes through repeatedly in his battles with Flacelière, director of the Ecole normale supéieure, the International Psychoanalytic Association, and the Société psychoanalytic de Paris (just to name a few). In a sense, Lacan used his role as teacher/performer to encourage student resistance and political action. In describing the cancellation of Lacan's seminar at the Ecole normale supéieure, Rabaté says,

> The last session of the seminar was devoted to scathing political remarks denouncing the director's double game, which led to a chaotic sit-in in his office, a fitting emblem of Lacan's conflicted relations with almost all official institutions. Lacan, following more in the steps of Chairman Mao, who repeatedly used the younger generations as a weapon against the old guard, than in those of de Gaulle, who had haughtily dismissed France as ungovernable, was no doubt starting his own cultural revolution (p. 6).

Lacan's role as teacher/performer depended on the collusion and support of his students. They had to believe in his re-reading of Freud as a necessary engagement of psychoanalysis and they also had to believe in him as the proselytizer of the "gospel." He goes so far as to say that because he returns to Freud's exposition of the unconscious and that the unconscious "tells the truth about truth," that he is speaking the truth about Freud (Écrits, 868). Lacan's reverence for Freud and his claims to be speaking the truth about Freud indicate his profound wish to be associated with Freud. He was indeed a Freudian and, in particular, one who staked his career on students' bequeathing upon him the same sort of reverence he gave to Freud.

As a teacher, Lacan reveled in being the point of reference and departure for his students. He was a mediator, of sorts, in their conversation with Freudian theory, psychoanalysis, and philosophy. He was, by all accounts, a dynamic mediator, one who embraced the question of "style" in both his writing and his life. Rabaté (2003), once a student at the Ecole normale supérieure, remembers that students viewed Lacan with awe, an almost star-like worship. They spoke of him being "driven to the school's entrance to emerge with a beautiful woman on his arm and make his way up to the office of Louis Althusser . . . Lacan was known to draw crowds from the city's select quarters, a medley of colorful intellectuals, writers, artists, feminists, radicals, and psychoanalysts" (p. 1). He was, in this sense, a public intellectual, one who inspired and provoked with his intellect and his personality.

As a public intellectual, he remained connected to multiple communities as he simultaneously rejected the hierarchy of certain institutions. Liu (2003) suggests that Lacan emerged as a pop star post World War II precisely because of his turbulent relationship with the International Psychoanalytic Association (from which he was eventually excommunicated) and his theoretical conflicts with other Freudians. Perhaps more importantly, Lacan became a public intellectual (in this sense, one who was known by the public) as he manipulated various forms of telecommunications to spread his messages. As Liu (2003) describes, "Playing the master on the airwaves allowed for Lacan to perform as both charlatan and master—consider his performance in *Télévision*: His analytic attitude seemed like a posture of pure provocation of his more conservative colleagues" (p. 253). Through media, Lacan spoke and he clearly expected for people to listen. Recast in cinematic imagery, he could enact his theories for different audiences and, in so doing, disseminate his re-reading of Freud. In truth, he could become the voice of Freud.

Lacan also used his pedagogy and his access to radio to disrupt the political climate of post World War II France. When the Ford Foundation rejected his proposal to translate Écrits into English, Lacan takes it not only as a personal affront to his theoretical interpretation of Freud, he sees the foundation's rejection as evidence of a much larger conspiracy on the part of America to shape/manipulate/refashion intellectual thought across the world. Liu (2003) describes Lacan's use of radio airwaves to voice his frustration at the rejection by the Ford Foundation by commenting,

> That he related the anecdote in a radio interview is all the more significant: weird as he was, he understood radio's function as a super-egoic voice. Radio transforms the voice into aural material that shakes us up because it seems to be audible everywhere, all at once. Lacan is chiding the leftist movement for its naïveté: the demand for 'an immediate effect' is part of a fantasy of political efficacy and critical resistance. He is warning his interlocutors that American institutions have an invisible political effect on post-war intellectual life, censoring and policing the translation of texts . . . (p. 258)

Even though the Ford Foundation was/is a philanthropic organization, Lacan called into question its motives in a very public way. And while his immediate impetus for charging the Ford Foundation with censorship may have been rooted in his frustration at the rejection, his charge that the foundation was using its influence to further a particular intellectual agenda would later come to light. According to Liu, the publication of Frances Stoner Saunders' *Cultural Cold War: The CIA and the World of Arts and Letters*, signaled the emergence of American philanthropic organizations into the political realm. These organizations were, according to Liu, "engaged institutionally and ideologically with the Central Intelligence Agency in the dissemination of an imperialist vision of post-war Europe, re-formed and re-structured under American domination" (p. 258). Lacan recognized this American imperialism as a cultural assault, an attempt to reconstruct French intellectual thought.

For Lacan, television was not the only medium by which he taught the world. Tape recorders consistently captured his voice as he gave his noted seminars. Students, of all ages and dispositions, could listen to his voice repeatedly. The tape recorder, in a sense, magnified Lacan's presence and rendered him safely stored to the annals of history. As Liu (2003) adds, "Lacan's feedback loop was plugged into the various low-tech media: the spontaneity and obscurity of his speech was guaranteed by the transcription that was made for his eyes only. His audience had to be all ears, or else smuggle in tape recorders of their own . . ." (p. 262). In these recordings, Lacan emerged as both ruler and captive; he licensed the recording, a recording which would confine his speech to reel/tape. In this confinement, people would try to pin him down, to continuously playback his recorded voice in an effort to solidify his arguments. It seems a strange contradiction, that this teacher who resisted being pinned down, would sanction the recording of his seminars, an act which would most definitely lead to others believing they had finally "caught" his meaning. But if we understand Lacan as a teacher who craved a particular reverence from his students and the public, then we can understand why audio and visual mediums attracted him so immensely.

Tape recordings and the transcriptions which would ultimately stem from them captured Lacan's interest for other reasons as well. His fascination with the slipperiness of language led him to make clear distinctions between the spoken and written word. In his speeches, he performed in more spontaneous ways. Written language could not reflect the same sort of improvisation. Liu (2003) best describes the tension inherent in transcribing Lacan's seminars when she remarks, "We can also recognize that transcription captures the spontaneity of the improvised and the extemporaneous in a pedagogical performance . . . the process of editing a transcription adds another layer of complexity to the attempts to reconstitute the unpredictability of the pronouncement" (p. 266). Without a doubt, Lacan's seminars were works in progress; his efforts to re-work them long after they were given proved that he appreciated both the spoken and written word. He used each for different purposes; the spoken word provided more freedom. It was, in a way, libratory. Writing, on the other hand, allowed him the space to solidify his thoughts, to attune himself to the specific difficulties of language, and to reconstruct it in purposeful ways.

Lacan's ultimate act as a teacher was to found his own school in 1964. He initially called it the Ecole Francaise de Psychanalyse and he later changed the name to the Ecole Freidienne de Paris. With this act of separation, Lacan distinguished himself as scholar, teacher, and politician. He would control all administrative and intellectual decisions for the school and, most importantly, he would serve as the primary pedagogue for the school. In creating his own mini-universe, he centered himself. This school would represent a special psychoanalytic space, a space in which he could bring together the clinical and the pedagogical. It would be a space that embraced unpredictability. Liu (2003) paints a picture of Lacan's psychoanalytic practice after the founding of his school (the EFP) by quoting, at some length, Roudinesco's description of Lacan's work as a clinician,

> . . . [T]the door at the rue de Lille was open to anyone and without appointment: to members and non-members, to analysands and the 'sick,' to robbers, thugs, psychotics, and the troubled…In sum, anyone could show up at his home to discuss absolutely anything . . . Very early on, Lacan contracted the habit of no longer giving appointments at fixed times. He was unable to refuse anyone and anyone could come to his sessions according to his whim or need. The Doctor's house was an immense asylum in which one could move about freely, its doors open from morning to night, among first editions, artistic masterpieces, and piles of manuscripts (p. 268).

In this environment, just as he had done in founding his school, Lacan situates the "Other," (the unconscious of his students). Just as he had emphasized Copernican theory as representative of the importance of re-centering the "Other," (the sun becomes the center of our universe rather than the earth), so does he, in his commitment to unpredictability, attempt to center the "Other," (or, in a more specific sense, the unconscious of his patients). His school and his practice reflected this complicated consistency of chaos.

THE THEORETICAL PREMISE OF THIS BOOK

As I stated at the outset of this chapter, I understand Lacan as an educator, one who blended his clinical practice with his teaching and public speaking in dynamic ways. I am an educator rooted in cultural studies discourse and, in that framework, I profess that our pedagogical practices should reflect democratic principles. Many researchers are now equating quality education with democratic education, a concept that grounds our constitutional government. These educators have argued that democratic education emphasizes engaged learning, is attune to issues of justice and equity, and is intricately connected to the "real world" (Apple, 1982; Carlson & Apple, 1998; Dewey, 1902 & 1932; Freire, 1998; Giroux, 1988; hooks, 1994 & 2003; Shapiro & Purpel, 2005; Spring, 2006). It is a concept of education in which democracy is about experience and process, one in which teaching and learning are forever linked—there is no latter without the former (Freire, 1998; West, 1999).

Democratic education is not politically neutral. It is always a political act, shaped by the moral and ethical attitudes of teachers, students, parents, and administrators. As Shapiro and Purpel (2005) state, "We believe that education is always (and everywhere) about the business of legitimizing and reproducing existing values, and ways of life—or about working to oppose them" (p. xiii). To understand schools as intricately connected to the real world is to understand that education should create more ethically and socially responsible citizens, citizens who are attune to the suffering in the world and who recognize the possibility of meaningful education decreasing that suffering. In this way, democratic education fosters spaces for discussion, debate, contestation and creation. It gives students unlimited opportunities for discovery and pushes us to challenge the current ways in which education is an alienating experience, particularly for students of color and students in poverty (Banks, 2002; hooks, 1994 & 2003; Kozol, 1991; Carlson & Apple, 1998; Martin, 1985).

In essence, I argue that, as democratic educators, we find ourselves dedicated to *process*—to renegotiating our theoretical understandings of what democratic education is. And, it means that we must claim/envision/create multiple subject positions which demand that the political not end at the personal (Carlson and Apple, 1998). I suggest that public education is democratic life, rooted in discourse and positioned through naming, critique, and deconstruction. As a democratic educator, I am committed to broadening our theoretical understanding of democracy in public schools and, in that spirit, I use Lacanian psychoanalysis, with its emphasis on language and identity, to deepen our notions of what schools could do to foster meaningful learning experiences for children.

NOTES

---

[1] We should also understand the mirror as symbolic of the reflective environment. Children learn to define themselves by "seeing" themselves in others, by gauging people's reactions to them, and forming a self identity outside of themselves. In other words, the child's self identity

CHAPTER 2

MIRRORING: REFLECTIVITY, IDENTITY, AND SUBJECTIVITY

If Lacan were to return today to examine the United States' system of public education, I suspect he would question the purposes of public education. As a student of history, he would have been well aware of the founding principals of our public education, from its tenuous Jeffersonian beginnings to the common school movement in the 1830's and to the school desegregation efforts of the twentieth century. If, in his return, he were briefed on the current state of U.S. education by any politician or policy maker, I suspect that he would suffer through a litany of quantitative data which would, naturally, highlight our immense progress in "leaving no child behind." He would hear of the closing of the achievement gap, increasing test scores, and standardization of curriculum. I suspect, however, that he would not hear of increasing disparities in school funding for schools/districts with high minority populations. I imagine it would take him some time and perhaps some personal investigation to discover that we are identifying students by proficiency scores rather than name. If he took the time, as I believe he would, he would also learn of the events of Columbine and Red Lake, school shootings by boys who used their schools as platforms on which to launch personal protests.

If Lacan were to return today, I believe he would say that students in U.S. schools are experiencing multiple identity crises, crises which represent the speaking of unconscious thoughts and desires. He would ask us, as educators, to talk about how we attune ourselves to the shaping of identity. How do we, in our teaching and practice, listen for the unspeakable? Or, how do we speak the unspeakable? And, if we have no answer for these corollary questions, we are not truly educating. For Lacan, the self is a complicated concept, one rooted in his belief that psychoanalysts in his era had misrepresented the self as only a conscious, speaking being. Lacan, in contrast, believed that our existence as "I" depended upon the subject of the unconscious. To ignore the unconscious then would be tantamount to inviting disaster. If we ignore the subject or "I" as the unconscious, then we assume that our actions are always conscious ones that we enact with clarity and purpose. Since Lacan believes that the unconscious drives our actions, he would envision schools as places of exchanges of the unconscious, places where someone (presumably the teacher with the student) needs to consistently work at reading and interpreting these exchanges.

Lacan's interest in the construction and development of self might allow us to reconsider the purpose of education. Various educational theorists have argued that we need to teach to the whole child[1] but they have presumed that we all know who the whole child is. While this may seem to be a simplistic statement, I believe it must serve as the beginning of any discussion of teaching. In our efforts to standardize the curriculum, we have focused intensely on redefining content. We have not placed similar emphasis on defining the child. While I am not suggesting that we can create a uniform conception of "child" that will give teachers the ability to know how every child will react to certain conditions or situations, I am suggesting that we must clearly identify each child as a social being, one who is and should be a "subject" of study. How can we educate without studying children?

THE MIRROR STAGE

In 1936 Lacan delivered his first lecture on the mirror stage. He cut short his talk at the 16th Congress of the International Psychoanalytic Association (IPA) after being interrupted by Ernest Jones who was, at the time, chairman of the conference proceedings. Lacan, feeling jilted by the interruption, refused to submit his paper for publication in the conference proceedings. Thanks to the faithful notes of Françoise Dolto, we have access to the text that Lacan delivered in preliminary form one month before the actual IPA conference. In it, Lacan outlined what would become one of his most often cited theories, that of the mirror stage and the development of self identity. This theory brings together Lacan's psychoanalytic training and his philosophy because he partners the "I" of the ego with the "I" of the philosophical subject (or the subject of mankind). In this way, he puts the unconscious in relationship—the subject is thus tied to other people and to history. It is contextualized by the environment that surrounds it even though it (the subject, the "I") may not be able to articulate this relationship.

To explain, I shall begin with a brief synopsis of Lacan's mirror stage theory. Lacan suggests that between the ages of six and eighteen months, a child learns to recognize her/himself in the mirror. The mirror is both a literal and figurative concept. It represents both the physical mirror and the environment as mirror (we see who we are in others). When the child recognizes her/himself in the mirror, s/he develops a self concept; s/he is no longer a disjointed set of limbs but comes together as a whole body. As Lacan says,

> It suffices to understand the mirror stage in this context *as an identification*, in the full sense analysis gives to the term; namely, the transformation that takes place in the subject when he [*assume*] an image—an image that is seemingly predestined to have an effect at this phase, as witnessed by the use in analytic theory of antiquity's term, 'imago' . . . But the important point is that this form situates the agency known as the ego, prior to its social determination, in a fictional direction that will forever remain irreducible for any single individual or, rather, that will only asymptotically approach the subject's becoming, no matter how successful the dialectical synthesis by which he must resolve, as *I*, his discordance with his own reality (Écrits, 94).

For Lacan, the mirror stage is critical because it is in this recognition of her/himself as a whole being that the child begins to construct a self identity in relation to the other objects or people in the mirror. Equally important, however, Lacan argues that the child's first recognition of her/himself in the mirror is an "othering." The child first sees her/himself as an other and then, later comes to identify the baby in the mirror as her/himself.

Let me attempt to explain this concept using a visual image. Let's pretend that we have a nine month old baby girl. Her name is María. We place baby María in front of a mirror and she giggles and tries to touch the baby in the mirror. We say, like most parents, "Look at yourself in the mirror María, that's you! Do you see yourself?" At this point, our little darling does not recognize herself. Despite our best efforts, she has no idea that the baby in the mirror is actually her. Now, let's imagine that baby María is fifteen months old. She sees herself in the mirror, touches her head, and notices that the baby in the mirror also touches its head. She is amazed. So, she tries something else. She touches her stomach. The baby in the mirror also touches its stomach! After a few more experiments, María comes to realize that the baby in the mirror is actually her. She then becomes fascinated with herself. She stands in front of the mirror and kisses her image. For Lacan, this moment of identification is critical because it marks a transition from "other" to "I."

Because we first see ourselves in the mirror as an other, as some other baby, we do not conceive of ourselves as a distinct and unified "I." Instead, we question/wonder why the baby in the mirror is as s/he is, why s/he looks like s/he does. Lacan says the baby in the mirror represents a specular image. The specular image is the one that we see or perceive. Lacan, in fact, says, "The specular image seems to be the threshold of the visible world, if we take into account the mirrored disposition of the *imago of one's own body* in hallucinations and dreams" (Écrits, 95). He goes on to add that this mirrored image, whether reflected in a physical mirror or in other people who look like us, gives us a false sense of being. Because a baby does not initially recognize the reflection in the mirror as her/himself, but sees or feels other people around her/him, the baby senses that s/he is a being like the others but can not articulate *why* s/he is like the others (or different from the others). Fink (2004) elaborates on this false sense of being,

> In the mirror stage, the ego is precipitated due partly to the tension owing to a lack of unity and coordination in ourselves. We sense that we are *not* beings like the other unified beings we see around us; there is as yet nothing we can point to as a discrete, total being (something that can be counted as a One). Instead, there is a conspicuous lack of being; being as such is missing prior to the anticipatory action of the mirror state (which creates a One where there was none). This is why Lacan tends to associate the ego with false being (p. 100).

For Lacan then, the mirror stage is critical in the construction of the ego or self identity. It marks the beginning of our move from false to social being (thinking of ourselves as the center of the universe) to understanding ourselves in relationship to others and the environment.

When a child recognizes her/himself in reflection, s/he moves from the specular to the social "I." At this point, the child becomes more than just an image. S/he becomes an image in a larger social context. What matters to the child is no longer just instinctual. It is visual and spatial. Once the child comes to understand and accept her/his reflective image as a self, then s/he begins to identify with or in contrast to the other images in the mirror.[2] Lacan explains this point by saying, "It is this moment that decisively tips the whole of human knowledge [*savoir*] into being mediated by the other's desire, constitutes its objects in an abstract equivalence due to competition from other people, and turns the *I* into an apparatus to which every instinctual pressure constitutes a danger, even if it corresponds to the normal maturation process" (Écrits, 98). Once we see ourselves in the mirror, we are no longer alone. We come to define ourselves as a part of a predetermined universe.

In recognizing ourselves in the mirror, we come to identify reality. We take note of how large or small objects are around us. We begin to determine what is important and what is not, to distinguish between what is necessary and what is desirable. We enter into a constant negotiation of lived reality. Lacan sums this up best by saying,

> The function of the mirror stage thus turns out, in my view, to be a particular case of the function of imagos, which is to establish a relationship between an organism and its reality—or, as they say, between the *Innewelt* and the *Umwelt* . . . the mirror stage is a drama whose internal pressure pushes precipitously from insufficiency to anticipation—and, for the subject caught up in spatial identification, turns out fantasies that proceed from a fragmented image of the body to what I will call an 'orthopedic' form of its totality—and to the finally donned armor of an alienating identity that will mark his entire mental development with its rigid structure (Écrits, 96-97).

For Lacan then, the mirror stage is marked by a particular constriction. The moment we recognize ourselves in the mirror is the very moment we begin to recognize the external reality which shapes our existence. We are no longer a nebulous collection of parts moving without regard. We are, instead, a unified whole that has limits. Just as our parts (limbs) are connected, we are similarly connected to and constrained by the world around us.

ALIENATING IDENTITY: SITUATIONAL AND MATERIAL REFLECTIVITY

If we continue with our analysis of Lacan's mirror stage, we must also consider the content in the mirror, the environment which the mirror projects. For the moment, let's consider the other people who might be reflected in the mirror. If baby María sees herself in the mirror with a parental figure (or someone else), she will notice that this person is looking at her. As a consequence, she will begin to see herself in relation to this person. She learns to identify herself as an "I" precisely because someone else is identifying her as such. This has profound implications for the construction of identity. It is, as Lacan terms, the beginning of the formation of an alienating identity, one that is created based partly upon the reflections/reactions of the parental figure(s) in the mirror.

In this sense, the emotional, psychological, or physical reactions that the parental figure(s) reflect in the mirror contextualize the child's interpretation of "I." If the reaction is one marked by love, care, or compassion, the child will begin to construct a self identity in reaction to those reflected emotions. If, instead, the reaction is one marked by disgust, hate, or apathy, the child will begin to construct a self identity in response to those. The child thus sees in the mirror a reflected relationship. It is a relationship that s/he is a part of yet it is also a relationship that allows the child to create an "I" beyond a sensory or instinctual awareness. It is a reflected image in which the child is both the creator and the created simultaneously. S/he generates a reaction from a parental figure and, in that reaction, the parental figure treats the child as a distinct and separate entity.

Thus the mirror stage signals the coming of consciousness for the child, a consciousness that is determined by the presence of someone else in the mirror with the child. It is a consciousness predicated on the assumption that there will be someone else in the mirror. And, once the child distinguishes between herself and the "Other" in the mirror, she constructs her self identity by "reading"[3] others. Fink (2004) describes the child's development of self consciousness in the following passage:

> According to Lacan, self-consciousness arises in the following manner: By internalizing the way the Other sees one, by assimilating the Other's approving and disapproving looks and comments, one learns to see oneself as the Other knows one. As the child in front of the mirror turns around and looks to the adult standing behind her for a nod, recognition, a word of approval or ratification—this is the reformulation of the mirror stage in Seminar VIII (Chapters 23 and 24) presupposed here—she comes to see herself as if from the adult's vantage point, comes to see herself as if she were the parental Other, comes to be aware of herself as if from the outside, as if she were another person (p. 108).

If we consider the implications of this othering, of the child learning to see herself from the adult's vantage point, then we come to understand why Lacan refers to the self identity (ego) created in the mirror stage as false being. Because the process of creating this "I" began with a disjointed sense of self prior to the mirror stage and because, in the mirror, the child develops a self identity through the eyes of someone else in the mirror, the self is really more of a projection.

For Lacan, the mirror stage came to symbolize less of an actual developmental stage and more of a process. Just as he understood the mirror as figurative and literal, so did he perceive the mirror stage to be a complex negotiation of identity which could not be reduced to a mere stage. According to Rabaté (2003), "In the context of Lacan's thinking, the idea of a mirror stage no longer has anything to do with a real stage or phase in the Freudian sense, nor with a real mirror. The stage becomes a psychic or ontological operation through which a human being is made by means of identification with his fellow-being" (p. 29). Lacan did, however conceive of the mirror stage as a process with a definitive beginning and ending. From his theory of the mirror stage, he postulates the idea of the subject, a theoretical construction of self that he distinguishes from the ego.

Ultimately, I suggest that the child's construction of self in relationship to other(s) in the mirror represents situational reflectivity. The image that the child develops of her/himself depends on the context of the situation presented in the mirror. Situational reflectivity demands that we ascertain how the mirror came to be and how people came to be in the mirror. The mirror, though physically constructed has a context, a history. The other(s) in the mirror have a context, a history that determines their position in the mirror. If these people are caregivers for the child, then they have a historicized understanding of the child. They can remember their relationship to the child. Context and history shape the relationship reflected in the mirror. Though the child may not grasp this context, s/he is inevitably tied to, created by, and reflected in circumstances that have a history. The mirror, for example belongs to a timeline; there is a story that explains it existence. How might that story reflect upon or impact the child's construction of self? We must also consider the context of the child's interaction with the mirror. How, why, and when the mirror is placed within the child's field of engagement (or vice versa) could have profound implications for the child's understanding of self. Whether or not the child encounters the mirror on her/his own, is placed before the mirror playfully, or left in front of the mirror in disgust would provide different encounters with the mirror and, possibly, different constructions of self.

If we consider situational reflectivity with a figurative mirror, then we can also understand how history and context affect our construction of a self identity. If there is no physical mirror, then our understanding of self is completely contingent upon the reaction of others and the response of other environmental conditions to our existence. Let's use an example here. If I have a physical mirror and I can see into that mirror, then I can see myself without another person in the mirror. Once I recognize that the baby in the mirror is a reflection of my image, and then if I encounter the mirror alone, I can interact with myself, observe myself in the mirror. If, however, there is no physical mirror or I have no sight, I rely more heavily on others to treat me as a whole and unified self.[4]

To push the concept of the mirror further, let's analyze the materiality of a literal mirror. The material contexts of the mirror are equally as important as the situational contexts. This I shall call material reflectivity. What kind of mirror is it? How is it framed and what condition is it in? Does its material condition reflect care or neglect and how might the child possibly interpret either case? Is it a large mirror that affords the child a wider physical context, and thus more possibilities for comparison when beginning to define the "I"? Or, is it a small mirror with limited scope and people with which to compare? And what if there is no mirror in the literal sense? Once the child recognizes her/himself in the mirror, then s/he will begin to scrutinize the other people in the mirror as well as the mirror itself. Although Lacan associated the mirror stage with Freud's concept of narcissism (the child becomes fixated with her/himself in relation to the other(s) in the mirror), other of Lacan's contemporaries suggested that the mirror stage was not based only on primary narcissism. Melanie Klein (as do I), for example, also focused on the importance of object relations in the construction of identity. Providing that the child does not develop a completely narcissistic personality, fixated on her/himself, s/he will begin to focus on the environment reflected in the mirror. And, later, the child will begin to question the construction of the mirror itself.

The mirror, in the literal and figurative sense, represents much more than a reflective place. When Lacan argues that the mirror stage represents the transition from the specular to the social "I," he interprets the mirror as a representation of the social world. In it, the child comes to see her/himself as engaged with others. In this stage, presence and absence are both equally important. What the child can see in the mirror can be interpreted. And what the child can not see also affects her/his interpretation. From the moment the child recognizes her/himself in the mirror, s/he begins an important journey towards becoming a subject. Lacan would emphasize the significance of this transition throughout his work. He would link the subject to Freud's topography of the id, ego, and superego by distinguishing between the "I" of the subject and the "I" of the ego. Lacan associated the "I" of the ego with consciousness and the "I" of the subject with the unconscious. This distinction would have tremendous impact on the field of psychoanalysis and our understanding of identity.

THE SUBJECT AND THE "I"

Though Lacan would never attribute his theory of the mirror stage to any one person, he did draw on the work of psychologist Henri Wallon. Five years before Lacan attempted to deliver his first lecture on the mirror stage, Wallon had developed a mirror test by placing a child in front of a mirror and watching the child gradually learned to recognize itself in the mirror. Rabaté (2003) posits the relationship between Wallon and Lacan's theories:

> In Wallon's view, the mirror test demonstrates a transition from the specular to the imaginary to the symbolic. On 16 June 1936 Lacan revised Wallon's terminology and changed the *épreuve du miroir* into the stade du miroir ('mirror stage')—that is, mixing two concepts, 'position' in the Kleinian sense and 'phase' in the Freudian sense. He thus eliminated Wallon's reference to a natural dialectic. (p. 29)

As Lacan further develops his theory, he sets himself apart from Wallon by emphasizing the unconscious in the construction of self identity. For Lacan, the mirror stage marked the emergence of the subject (of the unconscious) because the ego (conscious) would begin to understand itself as connected to and in conflict with people who are not always what they seem. Since the ego mediates between the Imaginary (self awareness), Real (the world that cannot be captured in language), and Symbolic (the world as represented by language) realms, the ego links the conscious self to the world through discourse.

Lacan, however, would suggest that the mirror stage is important because, in it, the child creates a self identity based upon unconscious desire (of the child and the other(s) in the mirror). S/he begins to believe that the "I" (of the ego) or the "I" of the conscious is the only "I." The child learns (through its observation of others) to reject unconscious desires and thus mistakes the "I" of the conscious as the one and only self. Campbell (2004) attempts to explain this point when she comments,

> For Lacan, the mirror stage can be understood *'as an identification'* which forms the ego-ideal and hence precipitates the ego. For Lacan, identifications are always situated in the imaginary order because they reflect the ego's narcissistic perceptions . . . Lacan argues that in imaginary identifications, the object is caught in the ego's *méconnaissance* or misrecognition of the other as a self. The ego misrecognizes the other in its specular reflections, perceiving the other as identical to itself. The identificatory object is known only as the same as self, and with that misrecognition comes a refusal of difference. In a desire for sameness, the ego perceives only those qualities that are identical to it, so that it refuses difference in the object. The identificatory object functions not as an Other but as an imaginary counterpart, an other that the self imagines to reflect it (p.101).

Because the child embraces the reflection in the mirror as its own, then it identifies as that reflection; it becomes that child. In doing so, the child focuses more on how s/he is like the child in the mirror rather than how s/he is different. By failing to see difference, the child develops a self concept that is unable or unwilling to accept unconscious desires that may contradict the perception that s/he is just like the reflection in the mirror.

Since the ego, according to Lacan, is unable to accept that unconscious desires define it, then it can not truly represent the "I." To capture the essence of the "I," Lacan uses the term subject. The subject recognizes that it is defined in the Symbolic order by language. In chapter 3 I will talk more about the significance of discourse to Lacanian analysis, but here, a brief explanation is in order. Discourse (or language) is governed by rules and works in patterned ways. These rules and patterns construct meaning for us. Lacan would argue that we enter the world through and with language. Language defines us; it allows us to define ourselves. The subject, then, only becomes a subject within language. And, because Lacan believes the unconscious is structured like a language, it manifests itself in patterned, although perhaps unpredictable, ways. Lacan believes the ego ignores these complexities.

As I stated before, the mirror stage represents a development of self consciousness, a coming to understanding of the self as a "thinking self." When the child learns to see itself in the mirror through the eyes of others, s/he begins to operate with a Cartesian sense of the world. The Cartesian[5] ego believes, "I think, therefore I am." According to Fink (2004), "The Cartesian ego assures itself it exists due to a consciousness that stands outside the ego that transcends the ego: a consciousness of consciousness or a consciousness raised to the second power..." (p. 109). It is important here to re-emphasize this Cartesian split because it is a western way of viewing the world that grounds our existence. Instead of following the Ubuntu logic, "I belong, therefore, I am," we develop a self consciousness based on the premise that thinking (or cognition) creates the self. In doing so, we foreground "logic" and background feeling or emotion.

In contrast, the subject claims no self knowledge. It can not consider itself an object of reflection because it is driven by the unconscious and the unconscious does not consider itself an "I." As a result, Fink (2004) says, "The subject may be dead and not know it, want something and not know it, and even speak without knowing it . . . The unconscious is not something *one* knows but, rather, something that is known" (p. 109). For Lacan, this would become the major distinction between the "I" of the mirror stage and the subject. In narcissistic fashion, the "I" of the mirror stage mistakenly assumes that it is a self. It presumes that because it sees itself "outside of the self," or through the eyes of others, that it has self consciousness. But Lacan would argue that this is a false consciousness, that we do not recognize our unconscious selves in the mirror and, without doing so, we cannot really know who we are. The subject, however, is not created by the mirror; it is created by language. And since the unconscious manifests itself through language, the subject is a better representation of who we really are.

Indeed, Lacan's belief that the unconscious was structured like a language[6] led him to suggest that the subject could never truly know itself. He goes so far as to query, "Once the structure of language is recognized in the unconscious, what sort of subject can we conceive of for it?" (Écrits, 800). Lacan puts forth the subject as a speaking subject, one that enunciates unconscious desires. He specifically says,

> I am merely referring obliquely to what I am reluctant to cover with the inevitable map of clinical work. Namely the right way to answer the question 'who is speaking?' when the subject of the unconscious is at stake. For the answer cannot come from him if he does not know what he is saying, or even that he is speaking, as all of analytic experience teaches us (Écrits, 800).

For Lacan, psychoanalytic practice is inextricably bound with the subject and the subject represents the unconscious through language. If the subject represents the unconscious through language, then the discourse of the subject is questionable, at best. We can never be sure if the words that we speak are truly indicative of the unconscious. They may, instead, reflect a poor representation of it.

To further explain his point, Lacan describes the psychoanalytic session as a space that interrupts false discourse. Since the speaking subject uses language that can not grasp the full intent of the unconscious, then the psychoanalyst cannot merely analyze the words that come forth in the psychoanalytic session. Lacan explains,

> Lest our hunt be in vain, we analysts must bring everything back to the cut qua function in discourse, the most significant being the cut that constitutes a bar between the signifier and the signified. Here we come upon the subject who interests us since, being bound up in signification, he seems to be lodging in the preconscious. This would lead us to the paradox of conceiving that discourse in analytic session is worthwhile only insofar as it stumbles or even interrupts itself—were not the session itself instituted as a break in false

> discourse, that is when the discourse realizes when it becomes empty speech . . . (Écrits, 801).

What is most important in revealing the subject then, is analyzing the interruption of language, looking at the thoughts/feelings which resist capture in words[7]. Lacan also compared empty speech [parole vide] to full speech [parole pleine]. In empty speech, we are unable to discern the subject's "real" meaning but in full speech we are. Lacan thus distinguishes between authentic speech and inauthentic speech. Žižek (2005) claims that we must recognize that the importance of empty speech is much more complicated than the difference between authentic and inauthentic meaning. Rather, empty speech is significant because, in it, language functions as a sort of password — as a way to understand true meaning. Empty speech is empty because, at any given time, its meaning could change, the password (or key to unlocking meaning) could shift. Žižek says, "And Lacan's point is that human speech in its most radical, fundamental dimension functions as a password: prior to its being a means of communication, of transmitting the signified content, speech is the medium of mutual recognition of the speakers" (p. 153). Speech provides for us a mutually understood code, a way of extrapolating and interpreting meaning.

The subject, in this context, comes to *be* in the space between empty and full speech. Lacan did not intend for us to dichotomize empty speech and full speech, but he did want us to understand that each depends on the other. As Žižek (2005) says, empty speech "creates the space for 'full speech,' for speech in which the subject can articulate their position of enunciation" (p. 153). In coming to full speech, the subject understands the void that exists in empty speech. S/he recognizes the fallibility of language and the possibility of misinterpretation. Misinterpretation, in the Lacanian sense, would begin with the subject's misunderstanding of empty speech for full speech. The subject, in this misinterpretation, would believe that her/his words represented authentic thoughts/feelings. But, the unconscious does not so easily present itself. In fact, Lacan would argue that, because of the difference between empty and full speech, psychoanalysts need to attune themselves to the speaking rather than the content. As Nobus (2003) argues,

> The reason for Lacan's 'subversion' of the classical psychological notion of the subject is that during psychoanalytic treatment the analyst is not supposed to be concerned with how the analysand wittingly and willingly presents him- or her self in the twists and turns of verbal productions, nor in the content of the analysand's speech (what somebody is saying), but in the fact that something is being said from a place unknown to the analysand (p. 61).

The psychoanalyst must question the place from where the subject speaks rather than the content of the message. Since Lacan emphasizes the subject as tied to discourse and representative of the unconscious, then the psychoanalyst must search for those interruptions (dreams, signs, symptoms, etc.) that would give clues to unconscious desires. Only when these desires are identified will the subject be able to engage in full speech.

Equally important, Lacan argues that the speaking subject comes into being in relation to other speaking subjects. In the context of psychoanalytic discourse, this is critical because it complicates the process of interpretation. First, the subject (or analysand) speaks. S/he does not know where s/he speaks from. The analyst must pay attention to the act of speaking rather than the content and look for particular interruptions in speech which may signal the presence of the unconscious. But, the analyst must also recognize his/her hearing as an act of interpretation. Nobus (2003) adds,

> Analytic treatment rests on the manipulation of the analysands unconscious thoughts and as such, it should reach beyond what is said and how it is being said, towards an investigation of where things are being said from and who, if anybody, is actually saying it. What the analysand says is but a semblance and cannot be disassociated from what the analyst hears in his or her own understanding of the words; the very process of saying is much more important than the form of the productions in which it results (p. 61).

Thus, in the analytic relationship, the subject who is speaking is being interpreted by another subject. In a sense, language brings subjects together just as it tears them apart. If we broaden this understanding to include more than the relationship between psychoanalyst and analysand, then we can begin to understand how difficult it is for a "subject" to come into being. Because the subject's "being" depends on the subject's spoken words and understanding of others, s/he exists as a perpetually interpreted being.

In the psychoanalytic relationship, however, this interpretive process happens despite a different set of problems. In this relationship, the analyst occupies a particular subject space, a space of presumed authority. By virtue of the very meaning of the term "psychoanalyst," we interpret the psychoanalyst to be one who possesses a certain kind of knowledge—the ability to help us know ourselves. This presents an interesting dilemma. As Žižek (1991) compares the role of the psychoanalyst to that of the detective, he says, "it is only on this account that the detective's 'omniscience' is strictly homologous to that of the psychoanalyst, who is taken by the patient as the 'subject supposed to know' (*le sujet suppose savoir*)—supposed to know what? The true meaning of our act, the meaning of the visible in the very falseness of the appearance" (p. 57). In simpler terms, we expect the psychoanalyst to occupy a specific subject position. S/he is supposed to, by nature of the role, be able to help us uncover the meaning of speech, dreams, and symptoms. The same is true of other professionals who possess certain "expertise."

These expectations are bound to language; words provide particular meaning. Because they do so, they define for us the nature of our relationships. We assume and yield authority to other subjects on the basis of titles and although these titles may come with the appropriate associative educational qualifications, the presumption that someone is "the subject supposed to know" is still problematic. If we continue with Žižek's comparison of the detective's role with that of the analyst, then we can better understand the Lacanian subject. He suggests that a crime scene is structured like a language, similar to the unconscious. Specifically, he claims,

> We could then specify the function of the detective *qua* 'subject supposed to know' in the following way: the scene of the crime contains a diversity of clues, of meaningless, scattered details with no obvious pattern (like 'free associations' of the analysand in the psychoanalytic process), and *the detective, solely on the means of his presence, guarantees that all these details will retroactively acquire meaning*. . .What we have at the beginning is a void, a blank of the unexplained, more properly the *unnarrated.* (p. 58)

The subject then, represents a complex blend of the narrated and the unnarrated, of the explained and the unexplained. The unconscious is the unexplained. Lacan would thus argue that the subject differs from the ego because the ego claims its existence solely on the basis of conscious interpretations, it cannot account for the unconscious. The subject, by contrast, exists in (and because of) the critical juncture between the conscious and the unconscious, between the unspoken and the expressed.

For Lacan then the subject's existence depends on there being a speaker and a listener. When the subject expresses her/himself, the listener's hearing of that expression determines the meaning that comes forth. And this determination is based on a multitude of other factors; the context of the situation determines the interpretation that comes forth. Because the psychoanalyst is the "subject supposed to know," s/he claims a position of privileged listening and is expected to possess the capacity to translate the speaking subject's discourse (Rabinovich, 2003). While this may be the expectation for the psychoanalyst, I argue that, in everyday relationships, we operate with similar ways of positioning subjects. We seek advice from others who are "supposed to know" just as we simultaneously remain skeptical about the ability of some to understand our specific predicament. The ego, or "I," in this sense allows us to function in society and to follow "normal" parameters, to coexist within specific cultural expectations. But, we recognize that our being is contextualized and dependent on the interpretations of others.

THE DECENTERED SUBJECT

The subject ultimately differs from the "I" of the ego because it is a decentered self identity. Unlike the ego, the subject cannot claim to know all there is to know about itself because it is driven by unconscious desires. Since Lacan believed the unconscious was structured like a language and that it manifested itself in dreams, symptoms, and other interruptions, he argued (as had Freud) that the subject could only reconstruct the unconscious (rather than uncovering or discovering it). If we admit that the self is driven by unconscious desires, then we can begin to understand why our actions may be unexplainable. Simply put, we have no idea why we do some things. But, if pressed for an explanation, we will provide one knowing that this explanation does not really capture the meaning behind our motives. We may not believe that our explanation is a lie, but we do know it does not represent the complexity of the story.

So, the most important question here is, "How do we know that we do not know?" How do we know that the verbal explanation we give does not fully explain our reasons? According to jagodzinski[8] (2002), "the subject cannot be grasped essentially in its Being. Lacan's formulation of the *objet a[uture]* (the unknown element which is the 'cause' of desire) is what is in the subject 'more than' in himself or herself . . . It is because of *objet a* that we hate or abject the Other—desire or need the Other—which asks us to respond ethically" (p. 87). If we return to the idea of the mirror stage and we picture again a baby in the mirror coming to recognize her/himself as a self through the eyes of other(s) in the mirror, then we can begin to understand how the baby's first identification then comes before (or on the cusp of) language. In these initial stages of self identification, the baby feels something. jagodzinski refers to this feeling as part of the affective domain and he situates Lacan's concept of the Real in this domain. Before a child knows through language and/or thought characterized by language, s/he knows through feeling, touch, or sight. And while the child may not be able to articulate love, hate, fear (or any number of other emotions) s/he feels the experience to be real.

This being then is an epistemological one rooted in our persistent search for knowledge and truth. As an epistemological concern, being is determined by language and emotions, both of which are products of time and history. With language, we witness the evolution of meaning; words mean something different in different cultures and different eras. We also accept that emotions evolve over time; a circumstance may incite fury in one moment and incredible sadness in another. For Campbell (2004), this evolution in language and emotion is a critical one because it displaces and situates the subject. She says,

> The Lacanian subject is thus a speaking being that is produced in language. Such a conception of subjectivity should not be misunderstood as a final stage in a teleology of the development of a unified and unitary identity. In a typical polemic against developmental psychoanalysis, Lacan argues against '[t]his mythology of instinctual maturation' (É, 59). He argues that the subject in the present is a re-presentation of the subject's past and future. Subjectivity marks a temporal structure which language produces (p. 32).

The subject, as a temporal one, is constructed in relationship to the past and the future. We do not and cannot present ourselves in the present without acknowledging the prior forces which shaped our existence. Nor can we ignore the future possibilities which will force us to construct particular identities. Also important in this understanding of the subject is that the subject is never a solid and complete being. It is always in a state of "re-presentation," of re-constructing self identity. We must understand that the Lacanian subject is a subject engaged in constant identity work and that this work is shaped by unconscious desires that are mediated by and explained through language.

Because the subject, in the Lacanian sense, is created through language and is driven by unconscious desires which often escape language, it is a decentered one. It is decentered because the "I" is relative and relational, bound by and with other mediating factors. It is not an "individual" operating with singular desires, but, rather, it is a social being whose relationships and temporality make it distinct. This concept of the subject forces us to reconsider the narcissistic notion of individual, the ego that views itself as the center of the universe and as separate from the rest of the world. We are not separate, even when we are alone, because we are historicized, shaped by past events that created the present into which we were born. For Lacan, the philosophical subject and the psychoanalytic subject are corollaries. They represent different subject positions, that of consciousness, analysand, and analyst.

Each of these subject positions reflects the complicated relationship between conscious and unconscious thought. Even when we think we know ourselves, we do not. As Campbell (2004) explains, "the knowing subject of consciousness confuses *ego*, *I*, and *subject* so that the knower understands its 'self' as the *I* of consciousness. The knower's confusion of *I* and *ego* misrecognizes the ego as self, and the self as subject, in a defensive operation that repudiates the unconscious" (p. 37). This subject situates itself in the Imaginary register because it bases its conception of self on the presumption that what it sees in the mirror is the self. It clings to this image as a true representation of self and refuses to accept any part of the unconscious. In contrast, the subject as analysand recognizes the unconscious and seeks to articulate its meaning/desires. In the analytic process, the analysand "brings into speech (that is, signifies) the Other of the unconscious" (Campbell, 2004, p. 37). In this way, the subject brings the unconscious into the Symbolic order (the order of language). And, finally, the subject as analyst occupies a critical position precisely because the analyst holds as her/his primary function the interpretation of the unconscious into the Symbolic order.

S/he is supposed to create space and possibility of the translation of the unconscious into language. But the analyst is also struggling with "re-presenting" her/himself. S/he must realize and acknowledge that the unconscious drives her/his interpretations; in this sense, analyst and analysand are interchangeable positions. The unconscious of the analyst enters the analytic space just as the unconscious of the analysand does, both are critical to the creation of meaning for each subject. I will go into more detail about the subject positions of analyst and analysand in Chapter 4 but, suffice it to say, this relationship grounds Lacan's subject theory.

Ultimately, Lacan's exposition of the subject pushes us to examine how we know ourselves. Do we every really know who we are? Can we translate the unconscious into discourse (the Symbolic realm)? And, if not, is our self knowledge always a false consciousness, one marked by narcissism? Will our self perception forever be a case of mistaken identity? In becoming a subject, we begin to understand that who we are is not what we present to the world. To know ourselves requires recognizing that what is most important are the interruptions in discourse, the symptoms of unconscious desire which disrupt our speaking. We must attune ourselves to the unspeakable, to that which we feel in the affective realm but cannot find the words for in the discursive realm. Like children who are beginning to learn the rules of communication, we must constantly strive to speak the "Real" in words that may not capture the raw instinctual quality of what we experience.

The subject is not linear, though bound in time, we must understand it as connected in multiple ways to the Real, Symbolic, and Imaginary registers. It is dynamic, meaningful, and susceptible. With each moment and with each word, the subject reacts to, against, or with exterior and interior forces. It concedes or resists, conforms or questions. And, in doing so, it cannot be static. In this way, the subject is *more than* the ego; it is more than the "I."

THE SUBJECT AND DEMOCRATIC EDUCATION

If we define democratic education as predicated upon engaged pedagogy, committed to social justice, and problem based, then we have to redefine education with the subject as central to educational discourse. How do we identify the child's instincts and unconscious desires? How do we recognize "behavior problems" as symptoms of inner fears, issues which the child cannot articulate into language? The current climate in U.S. education is one of accountability and while I do not deny the importance of standards and evaluation, I do question, "Where is the child situated in this discourse?" We claim that increased testing will allow us to measure how far 'behind" children are, but this statement presumes that the most important part of the child is her/his cognitive ability. And though I do not believe the cognitive and the affective are so easily separated, I do believe that Lacan's theory suggests we place similar emphasis on the child as a psycho-social being.

Somehow, the study of children is now solely a subject for psychologists and a practice that most often occurs outside of the traditional classroom. During my five years teaching high school, I never had any significant opportunities to observe, study, and evaluate children beyond the content of the courses I taught. The only evaluations my principal expected from me were entirely course driven. Occasionally, if a child displayed repeated "behavior problems," I would be called upon to attend an evaluation meeting with the school psychologist and guidance counselor. On more than one occasion, I attended these psychological evaluations and Individualized Educational Plan (IEP) meetings[9] to discuss children I did not actually teach because they needed a "regular education" teacher present and the child's referring teacher was not able to attend the meeting. Rarely was I asked to contribute any meaningful observations to these meetings. And, if I had been asked to do so, I probably would not have been able to because, as a teacher, I was not trained to study children. I was trained to teach children and, I argue, there is a significant difference although observing and teaching should inform the other.

If I were to return to being a high school teacher with a Lacanian perspective, I would distinguish more clearly between the time I took to teach children and the time I spent observing children. I would demand that I have time to record and evaluate my students' social interactions. I would also demand that a trained psychologist observe and study my students on a weekly basis and that we have time to meet collectively to discuss each student's social development. And, I would invite parents in to each meeting to provide additional perspective on the child's activities outside of the school. In this way, we could frame our analysis of the child's "progress" on more than her/his understanding of the course content. Instead, we would consider the child's knowledge as framed by the social rather than the social being peripheral to the child's acquisition of knowledge. And though numerous educational theorists have argued that we consider the whole child in teaching, these theories have not mandated a shift in the way we do schools; they have not translated into practical application. Simply put, there is no organized structure in place to evaluate students as psycho-social beings on a regular basis in schools. The Cartesian mind/body split permeates our educational system to the extent that we ignore the psycho-social entirely, unless, of course, the child behaves in a way that is not "normal." To know children, we must develop systematic ways of studying them in relationship to others.

NOTES

[1] John Dewey (1902 & 1915) and Maria Montessori (1967) argued that we needed to consider the child in context and make education connect to the child's life experiences. Children are not blank slates; they come with rich and varied experiences to schools. More recent cultural theorists (Banks, 2002; hooks, 2003; Nieto, 2004; Perry, Steele, & Hilliard III, 2003; & Tatum, 1997) argue that we need to consider the cultural position of the child in conjunction with the cultural climate of the school.

[2] Once again, I use mirror figuratively and literally.

[3] I am using the term reading here as would Paulo Freire (1998). As humans, we learn to read the word and the world. When a child develops a self conscious, s/he is beginning to learn to read the world or, in the Lacanian sense, to read others in the mirror.

[4] D.W. Winnicott (1971) elaborates on Lacan's mirror stage in his book *Playing and reality*. In it, he argues that the first mirror for a child is the mother's face (I would change mother to parental figure). The baby learns to read the reactions of the parental figure and begins to create a self identity on the basis of these reactions. Lacan does not use the mirror as Winicott, to refer to the mother's face, but I think Winnicott's idea is an interesting one to explore as well.

[5] Cartesian is a reference to René Descartes, French philosopher who is often referred to as the founder of modern philosophy.

[6] For Lacan, this would be redundant. He believed the unconscious was a language.

[7] Lacan was a structuralist and, as such, distinguished between written and spoken language. I will elaborate on this distinction in Chapter 3.

[8] jagodzinski does not capitalize his name.

[9] IEP meetings are meetings designed to evaluate students who have been diagnosed with learning disabilities. By law, these meetings are supposed to include a "regular education" teacher (the teacher who is not assigned to the child as a "special education" teacher). Regular education teachers teach course that are open to all students. Special education teachers teach courses designed for students with learning disabilities.

CHAPTER 3

SPEAKING THE SELF: LITERAL AND FIGURATIVE IMPLICATIONS FOR IDENTITY

NARRATIVES AND MYTHS

As a psychoanalyst, Lacan attuned himself to narrative; he listened to people's stories. In this capacity, he became an interpreter of words, translator of the unconscious, and examiner of truths. He also became a student of language, attracted to the lure of structural linguistics. He respected, almost revered, language as the medium through which the unconscious entered the Symbolic realm. And he consistently questioned the normative structure of language, its capacity to establish conditions for speaking and writing. Equally important, Lacan was fascinated by the interruptions in language, the breaks or departures from expected conversation. In these breaks or points of departure, he saw the potential for escape; these were points of different possibilities in language. They were signs that language, in all its rigid formality, still had spaces for contestation and re-creation.

Although Lacan would later rely more heavily on mathematical symbols to represent understanding of the psyche, he would maintain a particular connection to narrative and myth. Both Freud and Lacan used narratives from fiction or classical mythology but, unlike Freud, Lacan did not always use them to delineate his more difficult concepts (see—the Oedipus complex and Freud's use of the Greek tragedy to explain his theory). Many critics attacked Freud's theories precisely because they were so contingent upon these classical myths; they believed that where there were flaws in the myth and that here were flaws in the application of the myths to psychoanalytical theory (Leader, 2003). Narratives and myths have a historical context, a position from which they are told and heard. To apply them to other contexts opens up the dangerous possibility of them being misappropriated.

But, for Lacan and Freud, translating the unconscious into theoretical terms would prove difficult, to say the least. In this respect, classical myths/narratives held deep possibility; they could serve as a translating medium, a way to bring the unexplainable into conscious explanation. And, they could bring the unconscious, the unexplainable into the realm of lived experience even though this lived experience might "live" only in the text of a classical narrative. As Leader (2003) says, "In Lacanian terms, myth is inserted as a way of approaching the real, which resists symbolization. If a basic tenet of psychoanalytic theory is that there exists a nonsymbolizable and nonrepresentable aspect of human reality, it follows that attempts to access it theoretically will involve possibly discontinuous modes of presentation" (p. 36). In this sense, Lacan and Freud used myth to grapple with the ambiguity inherent in narratives. Myths would give, in practical ways, alternative explanations of reality and/or the varied interpretations of a singular circumstance.

Narratives/myths would appeal to Lacan because he worked in the realm of individual narrative creation—psychoanalytic patients would construct, revise, and reconstruct their own narratives in his presence. In this way, he was both participant and observer because his role as psychoanalyst invariably shaped the reconstruction of these narratives. According to Leader (2003), Lacan would come to compare his role to that of a shaman because "The shaman appeals to myth to reintegrate what a patient may experience as arbitrary and incoherent physical pain. The appeal to the symbolic system of myth can serve to situate this in a framework of meaning giving the patient a language in which to express his or her psychic state" (p. 38). Using this comparison, we can understand how the presence of the psychoanalyst, whether intended or unintended, would affect the structuring of the patient's narrative. Nevertheless, Lacan could not deny his role; his fascination with the unconscious compelled him to hear the narratives and to interpret.

Lacan also grounded his understanding of narrative and myth in the work of anthropologist Claude Levi-Strauss. Lacan would use Levi-Strauss' work to distinguish between the role of the shaman, who was interested only in the events of the present, and that of the psychoanalyst, who had to also consider the relationship between past and present. The patient's narrative could not be divorced from the past because its meaning derived from the complicated relationship between past and present interpretive contexts (Leader, 2003). In analyzing narratives and myths in tandem with psychoanalytic theory, Lacan studied the relationships inherent in and represented in each text. For him, the study of relationships in narratives would enhance and contextualize his theories.

SPEECH AND LANGUAGE

In September of 1953, Lacan delivered a paper at the Rome Congress held at the University of Rome's Institute of Psychology. The paper, entitled "The function and field of speech and language in psychoanalysis" illustrated his connection to Ferdinand de Saussure's linguistic theory. In the theory of structural linguistics, language conveys meaning and we understand this meaning through the interplay of signs. Signs are combinations of signifiers and signifieds. A signifier is the form that the sign takes while the signified represents the concept, the idea being illustrated. If, for example, we are driving down a particular street, we might see the word stop. The word "stop" is a signifier. It is the form of a word or its sound image. If we see the word stop on a stop sign, it becomes a signified or a concept. As a driver, we understand that we are supposed to press the brakes and stop the car. We interpret the signifier (word) and signified (concept) together as a sign. If the context of the situation changes, our understanding of the sign could change. If, for example, we encounter the word "stop" on a test, it means that we are to put our pencil down and cease working on the test — this representation has nothing to do with a car or its associative motions. Lacan believes that the meaning of a sign is "floating" (changing) until a sentence is completed. The sentence then represents the fundamental unit of meaning in language.

Lacan differentiates himself from Saussure's theory by suggesting that we pay attention to the relationship between signifiers, not signs. In this sense, words or sound images are the key to language and interpretation. For Lacan, the word itself, the signified, provided structure and, as Campbell (2004) explains, he positions the signified as "an effect of the signifier" (p. 34). To some extent, there is always a disconnect between signified and signifier, between what we say and what is interpreted (or what we think we say, what actually is said, and what is heard). These disconnections, ruptures, or interruptions are what intrigue Lacan because they represent the movement of the unconscious into the symbolic order. To further understand Lacan's theory of speech, I feel it necessary to quote, at length, from "The function and field of speech and language in psychoanalysis." In the text, Lacan says,

> Whether it wishes to be an agent of healing, training, or sounding the depths, psychoanalysis has but one medium: the patient's speech. The obviousness of this fact is not an excuse for ignoring it. Now all speech calls for a response. I will show that there is no speech without a response, even if speech meets with only silence, provided it has an auditor, and this is the heart of its function in analysis. But if the psychoanalysis is not aware that this is how speech functions, he will experience its call [*appel*] all the more strongly; and if emptiness is the first thing to make itself heard in analysis, he will feel it in himself and he will seek a reality beyond speech to fill the emptiness. This leads the analyst to analyze the subject's behavior in order to find in it what the subject is not saying. Yet for him to get the subject to admit to the latter, he obviously has to talk about it. He thus speaks now, but his speech has become suspicious because it is merely a response to the failure of his silences when faced with the perceived echo of his own nothingness (Écrits, 247-248).

Here, Lacan argues that the primary function of the psychoanalyst is to hear and interpret the patient's speech; by stating that the psychoanalyst has but one medium, Lacan leads us to believe that the psychoanalyst uses the patient's speech to translate her/his unconscious desires or motivations. What is most intriguing about his arguments, however, is his suggestion that silence, or the absence of speech, leads the psychoanalyst to use behavioral clues to access the patient's motivations and/or desires. By doing so, the psychoanalyst's speech becomes suspect—s/he speaks in an effort to bring the patient to speak. And, by doing so, implies that the patient is withholding information or not speaking truth(s).

What I find most compelling in Lacan's argument is his emphasis on the call of speech for a response. Here again, he focuses on relationship; speech implies that there is someone speaking and hearing. Speech necessitates a response, even if that response is silence. And the response comes from someone other than the speaker. To speak then is to be in or request a relationship. With this understanding, we can push Lacan's analysis further and examine his belief that speech or language was not, could not be, neutral. To put an idea into words is to put it into context, to give it meaning, and to attempt to convey that meaning. As Campbell (2004) states,

"Lacan rejects the classical model of truth as *adequatio rei et intellectus*, that is, as a relationship between the idea and the object. In the Lacanian model of knowledge, there is no possibility of a neutral representation of reality precisely because to describe an object involves representing it in language" (p. 35). Speech, in this sense, represents a complicated relationship between sound and silence, between words and responses.

Speech is important insofar as it represents a changing relationship between signifiers and signifieds. Because Lacan's concept of the signifier and signified is a difficult one, I will spend a bit more time here elaborating on his explanation of the relationship between the two. As I said before, Lacan believed that the signified was an effect of the signifier; this could otherwise be rephrased as the signifier having a meaning effect. Between the word and the concept, meaning is created. At this point, Lacan distinguished his theory from Saussure because Saussure had argued that the relationship between the signifier and signified was arbitrary. Lacan, in contrast, did not believe the relationship was arbitrary. He felt that meaning effects did have some relationship to that which caused them but that we are unwilling to accept the relationship between signifier and signified because we want the cause to somehow represent or approximate the Real (that which can not be captured in language).

Let me pause here and give an example. If we were to say, "at some time," we would not believe that the words or the sound image would have anything to do with the meaning of the phrase. In this example, the phrase "at some time" is the signifier and the meaning we interpret from it is the signified. In Lacan's interpretation, the relationship between the sound of "at some time" and its meaning is not an arbitrary one (Encore, 23). Instead, he says, it has no meaning effect, that sound image itself bears no effect on the slipperiness of the meaning of the term. To have no effect is different from being in an arbitrary relationship. To be arbitrary would suggest that we could not explain the relationship.

EMPTY SPEECH AND FULL SPEECH

In "The function and field of speech and language in psychoanalysis," Lacan distinguishes between empty speech and full speech. Let us return to the quote, "This leads the analyst to analyze the subject's behavior in order to find in it what the subject is not saying . . . He [the analyst] thus speaks now but his speech has become suspicious because it is merely a response to the failure of his silence, when faced with the perceived echo of his own nothingness" (Écrits, 248). Lacan goes on to add,

> But, what in fact, was the appeal the subject was making beyond the emptiness of his words [*dire*]? It was an appeal to the truth at its very core, through which the calls of humbler needs vacillate. But, first and from the outset it was the call of emptiness itself, in the ambiguous gap of an attempted seduction of the other by means in which the subject manifest indulgence, and one on which it stakes the monument of his narcissism.

Many theorists have incorrectly assumed that empty speech [*parole vide*] and full speech [*parole pleine*] are direct opposites and that empty speech is inauthentic while full speech is authentic. The distinction between them is more complicated. As I stated in Chapter 2, empty speech can function as a sort of password, as a key to unlocking meaning. In this respect, the word or phrase actually enunciated may have nothing to do with the "true" meaning it conveys. A password, however, can give us access to an entirely different world of meaning.

Žižek (2005) elaborates on empty speech and full speech further by suggesting that empty speech creates the space for full speech. In this sense, full speech does not fill a void; rather, it creates the conditions for authentic expression. In this space, the subject can articulate "their position of enunciation" or the position from which they speak (p. 153). Only with/in empty speech can we ever really know who we are because it is here that we can actually realize our subject position(s). In Žižek's words, "In order to posit the substantial content as 'my own', I must first establish myself as a pure, empty form of subjectivity devoid of all positive content" (p. 154). To claim a particular subject position, we must understand the significance of empty speech as necessary to the construction of subjectivity. Empty speech creates the space in which we can find the words to identify ourselves, to speak ourselves, and to be ourselves.

WRITTEN TEXT

In "Encore, The seminar of Jacque Lacan Book XX," Lacan spends considerable time addressing the "function of the written." Lacan begins this part of the seminar with what he calls an admission. Having already published *Écrits* (a seminal collection of his work) he makes this comment,

> I am going to enter very slowly into what I have reserved for you today which, before beginning, strikes me as rather reckless. It has to do with the way in which we must situate the function of the written in analytic discourse. There is an anecdote to be related here, namely, that one day, on the cover of a collection I brought out—*poubellication*, as I called it—I found nothing better to write than the word *Écrits*. It is rather well known that *Écrits* cannot be read easily. I can make a little biographical admission—that is exactly what I thought. I thought perhaps it goes that far, I thought they were not meant to be read. That's a good start. (29)

In this self admission, Lacan points to his distrust of language, particularly the written word. He believes it confines his ideas and constructs them in a particularly rigid way, one that does not allow for ambiguity. But, here he also begins to illuminate the relationship between speaking, writing, and reading. He goes on to clarify this point by saying, "If there is something that introduces us to the dimension of the written as such, it is the realization that the signified has nothing to do with the ears, but only with reading — the reading of the signifiers we hear. The signified is not what you hear. What you hear is the signifier" (Encore, 34). In other words, we read meaning into words and this reading is more important than the specific sound image that is produced. As a matter of fact, it is precisely because we read meaning into/onto signifiers that we may not actually hear what was said.

This connection between speech and written language would be one that Lacan agonized over for much of his life. As one who was grounded in a philosophical and historical understanding of psychoanalytic theory, his fascination with speech and written text should come as no surprise. Perhaps Fink (2004) puts it best when he says, "My sense is that Lacan was striving to create a new audience with much of his work, a new breed of analyst-critics adept at reading both the analysand's discourse and literary texts (which have a tendency to become intertwined to a greater or lesser extent in many cases)" (p. ix). For Lacan then, all speech was like a text, to be read, deciphered, and interpreted. And this was an unavoidable process (for all) but one to which psychoanalysts were particularly attuned.

Writing, for Lacan, implied capture/captivity. It represented an imperfect attempt to grasp the meaning of speech in "the letter" and by letter, I mean written symbols. When Fink (2004) began his text *Lacan to the Letter*, he says,

> A friend and former teacher of mine, Richard Klein at Cornell University, once remarked that hardly anyone working on Lacan took the trouble to explicate his texts at length, preferring, apparently to comment on his theoretical apparatus rather than on his actual writing. The remark immediately struck me as true, and I realized that it applied to my own publications as well. The present volume is a first attempt to take up the implicit challenge: to take Lacan at his word, to read his texts *á la letter*—that is, both literally and to the letter (p. vii)

For Fink, this entailed grappling with Lacan's obscure French, his purposeful play on words, and his juxtaposition of particular phrases. Fink refers to his analysis as a literary one, one that demands particular attention to Lacan's word choice. It requires that Fink presume Lacan wrote what he meant to write, that his terminology was carefully selected with reason. And herein rests the problem with transforming speech to written text. It requires a certain set of presumption, 1) that the speaker said what s/he meant, 2) that the written words selected actually represent that spoken meaning, and 3) that the reader shares as similar discursive knowledge, that s/he will most likely correctly interpret the intended meaning. These presumptions are problematic, at best. Any writer knows that, sometimes, words cannot capture the essence of an experience and that, when chosen to represent that experience, words may convey a different meaning. With the translation of Lacan's French texts to English, we develop a new set of problems—most of which can be summed up by saying that translation is imprecise. In translating across languages, we inevitably misinterpret phrases—our language cannot quite grasp the full meaning of certain terms. Lacan would spend his entire life believing he was somewhere in the middle of spoken and written language. In this sense, his expression took place in a sort of purgatory, an in between place.

When Lacan attempts to explain the function of the written, he thus prefaced his comments with statements which indicated his reluctance to formulate some sort of systematic explanation. To do so would contradict his notion that theory existed in constant flux, perpetual states of re-presentation. He spends considerable time situating himself in his theory and using his life experiences as a context for his writing. To provide an example, I turn once again to "Encore: The seminar of Jacques Lacan Book XX." In Chapter II, "The function of the written," he says,

> A letter is something that is read. It even seems to be designed as a sort of extension (*prolongement*) of the word. It is read (*ça se lit*) and literally at that. But it is not the same thing to read a letter as it is to read. It is quite clear that, in analytic discourse, what is involved is but that — that which is read, that which is read beyond what you have incited the subject to say, which, as I emphasized the last time, is not so much to say everything as to say anything, without worrying about saying something stupid (*des bêtises*) . . . That is what I check when I look back, which I never do without trembling, at what I have proffered in the past. That always makes me awfully afraid, afraid of having said something stupid, in other words, something that, due to what I am now putting forward, I might consider not to hold up. . .Nevertheless, this 'rereading oneself' (*se relire*) represents a dimension that must be situated in relation to what is, with respect to analytic discourse, the function of that which is read (*ce qui se lit*) (29-30).

Here, Lacan distinguishes between reading the letter and reading. To read involves a much more complicated effort to interpret more than discourse. For Lacan, reading demands attention to what one said, one's current expression, and the context between each conversation. We must read to begin to understand our functions as subjects in language. Re-reading allows us to identify our subject position, the place from where we speak. It also allows us to determine if what we said in the past was a clearly articulated subject position. In addition, we can re-examine that articulated subject position from a distance and, from this distance, determine if we actually spoke what we intended to speak. Such a re-reading is critical because, for Lacan, it reflects one's understanding of discourse as contextual, interpretive, and positioned.

Lacan goes on to add that writing stems from discourse and, as such, can never quite accurately capture the full meaning of discourse. Specifically, he says, "Everything that is written stems from the fact that it will forever be impossible to write, as such, the sexual relationship" (Lacan, 1975, 36). Writing is an approximation, an attempt to reach meaning, but a stalled attempt nonetheless. It is an effort to solidify speech into the letter, but, for Lacan, the letter is "an affect of discourse" (1975, 36). What makes writing so tantalizing, however, is the possibility to give it different readings, to suggest different meanings of the signifiers.

THE FOUR DISCOURSES

Lacan theorized that there were four primary discourses — that of master, university, hysteric, and psychoanalyst. The discourse of the Master represents the discourse which creates the subject; it is the discourse which grounds all others.

The discourse of the university frames the subject's knowledge but this discourse can not capture the truth of the unconscious. The Discourse of the Hysteric reflects a search for the truth of the unconscious. The Hysteric's speech paves the way for the presentation of unconscious thoughts and, ultimately, creates space for the intervention of the psychoanalyst. The discourse of the Analyst brings knowledge into the space of truth. In this discourse, the subject comes to realize/recognize the Master signifier as its creator and speaks the truth based on this knowledge. Each of these discourses suggested different positions of the subject. And, as such, they represented vastly different ways of knowing. Lacan also believed that discourses were made up of signifying links and that these signifying links were actually relationships between signifiers. Lacan felt that these relationships or signifying links created a certain structure in language and, even if signifiers could take on different contextualized meaning, there was still a particular stability in language that allows us to understand one another. Equally important, Lacan maintained that discourse came through speech; written language is the material representation of speech. There is, therefore, a distinction between what we say and the material symbolization of that saying.

If we return to Lacan's idea that speech is intersubjective, that it requires a hearing subject, then we can understand how discourse would also represent this intersubjectivity. Discourse establishes and requires a social bond between subjects. As Campbell (2004) sums up,

> For Lacan, language produces a 'speaking being'—*l'être parlant*—and the relation between such subjects. In this way, the term 'discourse' implies a relation between speaking subjects. It represents the transindividual aspect of language that structures social bonds. The Lacanian concept of discourse links the structure of signification and the intersubjective relation because it describes signifying chains that form relations between subjects (p. 49).

Using this understanding of discourse, we can see how language determines social relationships as it simultaneously structures the nature of those relationships. Normally, we believe that we, as individuals, determine the nature of our own relationships, but Lacan's theory suggests that we are social beings, created in relationship by and through language. In a sense, we "fit into" discourse.

To frame Lacan's discussion of the four discourses, I must begin by discussing the schema he uses to describe the relationship between them. In this schema, he lays out the following: the master signifier (*le signifant maître*), knowledge (*le savoir*), surplus *jouissance* (*le plus-de-joir*), and the subject (*le sujet*). According to Campbell (2004), "the master signifier marks the subject's position within the signifying chain and hence within the discursive social tie," knowledge represents the "subject's knowledge" and the "form of knowledge of the subject, such as the differing conceptions of the subject within the university and psychoanalysis" (p. 50). She goes on to say that jouissance is the leftover of discourse; it is that which cannot be subsumed into language. And, finally, the subject is the subject of the unconscious, the object of study for psychoanalysis.

In "Encore: The seminar of Jacques Lacan Book XX," Lacan maintains that these discourses each operate in distinct and unique ways (21-22). These operations are marked by the terms, agent (*l'agent*), other (*l'autre*), truth (*la vérité*), and production (*la production*). The agent occupies the position of speaking subject, the "other" is the person to whom the agent speaks, "truth" is the truth of discourse, and production represents the outcome of discourse, the product of the discursive relationship between the agent and the other (Campbell, 2004, pp. 50-51). Each of the four discourses (Master, University, Hysteric, and Analyst), represents a different relationship between the agent, other, truth, and production. Lacan explains this difference through several rather complex diagrams which I will not elaborate on here. But, suffice it to say, each of the four discourses represents a different subject position and this position determines the subject's speaking relationship to the "other." In addition, the relationship between the subject position and "other" determine the "truth" produced in each discourse; hence, each discourse will operate differently and create a different product[1]

Ultimately, Lacan argues that any movement between discourses represents an affect of the psychoanalytic discourse. In a more basic sense, psychoanalysis can push the subject towards a different subject position. When describing his theory of the four discourses, Lacan takes a break to emphasize the following point,

> Well I would say now that there is some emergence of psychoanalytic discourse whenever there is a movement from one discourse to another. To apply these categories, which are structured only on the basis of the existence of psychoanalytic discourse, one must pay careful attention to the putting to the test of the truth that there is some emergence of analytic discourse with each shift from one discourse to another (pp. 20-21).

Since the object of psychoanalytic study is the subject of the unconscious and the "subject" in Lacan's four discourses is the subject of the unconscious, psychoanalytic discourse can affect a shift in subject position. And this shift changes the dynamic relationship of the different operative conditions of discourse; the agent projects in a different voice to the other, brings forth a different truth, and repositions the product of discourse.

Lacan believed that the discourse of the Analyst could prompt a re-reading of the subject. But, this re-reading was problematic because it presumes that the subject of the unconscious can either read itself or learn to read itself. And here, Lacan once again makes a connection between reading, writing, and discourse. He argues that the discourse of the analyst assumes that it can teach the subject to read, but that, even if it can, what the analyst teaches the subject to read, "has absolutely nothing to do, in any case, with what you write of it" (1975, 38). Here again, there is little connection between reading and writing because, the subject of the unconscious is difficult to pin down, to put into words. There is a literal and figurative statement here. In the literal sense, the letters the analyst will use to describe or explain the subject have nothing to do with the speech that has come forth from the subject's discourse. Figuratively, the analyst attempts to teach the patient to read the unconscious, but s/he must still rely upon that which the subject speaks or interprets. There is no way to unequivocally know if what the subject speaks and what the analyst interprets is actually the subject of the unconscious.

Ultimately, Lacan is not so much concerned with the "I" of the analytic discourse as he is with the place from which the discourse comes. Analytic discourse has a special relationship to speech. In speech, the important distinction was between the signifier and signified. The same distinction is not pre-eminent in written text. Instead, Lacan argues that "The signified is not what you hear. What you hear is the signifier. The signified is the effect of the signifier" (1975, 34). He goes even farther and says, "What is written is not to be understood" (35). There is no specific connection between spoke and written word other than the written word is an attempt to define the undefinable, to specifically articulate that which cannot be confined to the letter — the subject of the unconscious.

METAPHORS

If we return to Lacan's emphasis on signifiers (words, sound images), we must also examine his analysis of metaphors and their subsequent role in language. In "The instance of the letter in the unconscious," Lacan suggests that the field of the signifier is constituted by metonymy and metaphor. Metonymy represents the "word to word" connection between signifiers. Lacan uses as an example the words "ship" and "sail." He says that the link between theses two words is entirely contingent upon the signifier (or what we hear as the signifier). Metaphor, on the other hand, is important because it can create more ambiguous meaning. Lacan says,

> Metaphor's creative spark does not spring forth from the juxtaposition of two images, that is, of two equally actualized signifiers. It flashes between two signifiers, one of which has replaced the other by taking the other's place in the signifying chain, the occulted signifier remaining present by virtue of its (metonymic) connection to the rest of the chain. *One word for another*: this is the formula for metaphor, and if you are a poet you will make it into a game a produce a continuous stream, nay, a dazzling weave of metaphors (Écrits, 507).

Metaphor is exciting because it replaces one word for another and the signifying chain continues. In fact, Lacan seems most fascinated by this fact, that one word can replace another and the signifying chain continues without disruption. The ability to replace one word for another without causing a break in the signifying chain is reflective of poetic energy because, in a sense, one has created meaning from non-meaning — used a word which means something entirely different to articulate a specific point. In this way, metaphor proves that language falls in the realm of the Symbolic and not the Real. Because words can so easily replace others, their meaning can shift; it shifts because the Real is illusive, impossible to put into words.

More importantly, metaphor relates to the position of the subject (whereas metonymy relates to the position of the ego). Lacan is concerned with the intersection of subject and ego positions (if, indeed, they ever do intersect). Can the one ever replace the other in a *word-to-word* connection? Fink's (2004) analysis uses selections from Écrits. Using the following quote from Lacan (516-517), "Is the place that I occupy as subject of the signifier concentric or eccentric in relation to the place I occupy as subject of the signified? That is the question," Fink says, "the question is whether or ne'er the twain shall meet" (p. 102). Lacan's ultimate question is whether or not the subject who speaks is the same as the subject about whom it speaks. Or, put another way, when I speak, is the me that is speaking the same as the me to whom I am referring?

By questioning the position of the subject of the signifier and signified, Lacan begins to complicate the question of cognition. Descartes had argued, "I think, therefore I am." Fink suggests then that Descartes' notion of cognition positioned itself in the intersection of signifier and signified. Lacan, in contrast, argued, "I am thinking where I am not, therefore I am where I am not thinking" (Écrits, 517). Fink thus concludes that Lacan is saying the unconscious thinks, but that it thinks from an unknown place, a place where it is not. Using this logic, Lacan would suggest that the symptom is a metaphor; it is a metaphor for the unconscious. If we accept that the unconscious is thinking and that it is thinking from a place we cannot yet define, it can only be explained by a word/phrase that seemingly has no relation to it—a metaphor.

Lacan's most well known use of metaphor would appear in his usage of the Borromean knot. It was, literally, a knot formed by three linked rings. He would use this knot to further explain his theories; the knot would represent interlocking entities, in particular, the connectedness inherent in sentences. Lacan explained,

> But, still, what are we to do with this Borromean knot? My answer to you is that it can serve us by representing a metaphor that is so often used to express what distinguishes the use of language—the chain metaphor. Let us note that unlike rings of a string, the elements of a chain can be forged. It is very difficult to imagine how—one bends metal to the point where one can solder it. No doubt, it's not a simple prop, for, in order to be able to adequately represent the use of language, links would have to be made in that chain that would attach to another link a little further on with two or three floating intermediate links. We would also have to understand why a sentence has limited duration. The metaphor cannot tell us that (1975, 115).

The Borromean knot had continuity; it did not have a definitive beginning and ending. It could not serve as a direct representation of language because language has entry and exit points, places where sentences begin and end. In addition, Lacan emphasized the dependency inherent in the knot; if the knots were pulled apart, the chain would not exist. The same is typically true for sentence construction. If part of the sentence is removed, it loses its meaning. But, this is not always and unequivocally true. There are times when words can be removed from a sentence and it retains its coherence. The knot, on the other hand, could not claim the same ability. So while Lacan would use the knot as a metaphor for language, he also questioned its usefulness in this regard.

Ultimately, Lacan's fascination with language led him to use language in creative ways, to illuminate its complexities and challenges. He viewed language as the primary medium of psychoanalytic study but realized that the unconscious would not be so easily captured in language. For this reason, he equated symptoms with metaphors and analyzed them as symbolic of unconscious thought. And, at times, he used narratives and myths to explain his more complicated theories. Lacan was both a student and model of discursive strategy. He consistently looked for ways to manipulate and re-fashion discourse, to pull from it different possibilities. And what he valued most was the infinite possibilities inherent in unconscious thought; to recognize the unconscious and bring it into conscious discourse was the primary role of psychoanalytic processes.

LACAN, LANGUAGE, AND CULTURAL STUDIES

Lacan's exposition of language, his emphasis on metaphor, myth, and narrative, have exciting implications for the field of cultural studies. Edgerton (1996) claims that cultural studies is a translation across academic and non-academic discourses and across disciplines. Citing Hall (1990), Edgerton says that cultural studies "involves appropriation not just rejection. From this point of view cultural studies is a process, a kind of alchemy for producing useful knowledge. Codify it and you halt its reactions" (p. 22). In this regard, cultural studies represents a way of viewing/thinking/analyzing that draws from multiple disciplinary fields (history, anthropology, sociology, to name a few) and, in this process, critiques normative notions of culture and power. As a student and teacher of cultural studies, I am drawn to its possibilities for disrupting dominant discourses and re-writing curriculum. And, similar to Lacan, I believe language serves as the primary medium through which we learn to uncover multiple truths.

I am compelled by Edgerton's (1996) work because she emphasizes cultural studies as an effort in translation — it requires particular attention to people's lived experiences and the ways in which they talk about those experiences. As a cultural studies critic, however, my work is also deeply grounded in the works of Stuart Hall, Henry Giroux, Peter McLaren, Paulo Freire, bell hooks, Joe Kincheloe, Shirley Steinberg, Svi Shapiro, Kathleen Casey, Derrick Bell, and Adrien K. Wing. In many ways, their works intersect to create an educative matrix informed by critical pedagogy, feminist theory, and critical race theory. Lacan's critique of discourse is particularly applicable to cultural studies because it brings back to the forefront the problem of language. For cultural studies this problem remains — how do we construct and critique dominant discourses without creating a dominant discourse of our own? How do we define ourselves and what we do without succumbing to the limits of that definition? And, how do we establish our critique as a legitimate discourse in the academy without creating another canon of "great" authors?

To frame a beginning response to these questions, I will use Lacan and his juxtaposition of myth and narrative with psychoanalytic theory. In using myth and narrative, Lacan demonstrated a fundamental belief in the power of storytelling.

Stories, no matter the vantage point from which they are written, provide a framework for understanding. Stories can serve as metaphors for our own lived experiences and, by using them, we can begin to speak the unspeakable because through the story, we create distance. The truth of our pain is not so personal if we experience or speak it through another narrative. In this way, narratives can serve as metaphors for lived experience, as a way to understand that which we may not be able to personally claim.

Cultural studies theorists rely on narratives to dismantle dominant discourses. And while there are multiple variations of these dominant discourses, the most pervasive are 1) white privilege, 2) patriarchy, 3) sexism, and 4) heterosexism. What makes these dominant discourses so dangerous and powerful is their invisibility; most people do not realize that societal structures reinforce particular discourses. When Peggy McIntosh (2003/1988) put forth a systematic exploration of white privilege, she compared it to an "invisible knapsack," a system of unearned privileges that she enjoyed solely on the basis of her skin color. Such systems perpetuate precisely because they are invisible and, therefore, difficult to critique/challenge/dismantle. Edgerton (1996) argues that the dismantling of dominate discourses (or, at the very least, a shifting of) can happen with the interjection of narratives from marginalized groups. She is, in particular, speaking to the challenges of curriculum reform. She says,

> Literary works of marginalized groups can provide a passage to a shifting of discourse away from conceptions of multiculturalism as something we 'add on' to the curriculum, 'do for' marginalized groups, or as a means to simply 'change attitudes.' Such a shift away is a shift toward a more fluid and thoughtful 'discourse of encounters' in its abrogation of the problem of representation—representation as it concerns such entities and notions of identity, culture, and civilization—and in its problematization of notions of cultural translation (p. 6).

When used with specificity, with the specific goal to disrupt, the narratives of marginalized groups can intersect with dominant discourses to create new spaces for contestation. In these interstices, alternative narratives can impede the dominant way of thinking and speaking and, in this impediment, change the meaning of the discourse (if, only slightly). And while there is always the danger that the alternative discourse might be subsumed by the dominant one, the possibility of permutation still remains.

I believe that Lacan's significance to education is analogous to the relationship between cultural studies and translation. He was compelled to investigate and/or uncover the unconscious and he believed speech was the primary medium through which he could do so. We could characterize the unconscious, as the often ignored part of the psyche, as marginalized. But because it is what drives us, pushes us towards certain behaviors and actions, the unconscious is what centers us, what grounds our identities. Similarly, marginalized groups are critical members of society, many times they are the people most often ignored. Their voices, however, are most important to establishing any sort of collective understanding. Freire

(1970) would explore the relationship between the oppressed and the oppressor and he would conclude that only the oppressed could liberate themselves and the oppressors. Since the oppressor could not (or refused to) "see" the world of the oppressed, they could never act as the primary liberators. Only the oppressed, who experienced both worlds, could find the counter-hegemonic spaces to disrupt the system of domination.

Freire (1998b) was equally interested in language and literacy. His literacy programs for poor farmers in Brazil were founded on the belief that literacy was the medium through which the oppressed could politically act. They had to learn the language of the oppressor to be able to manipulate, reject, or recreate that language. He argues that reading the "word" is necessary for reading the "world." More specifically, he says, "The reading of the word, also a function of a search for text comprehension and thus of the objects contained therein, directs us now to a previous reading of the world" (p. 19). He goes on to say, "I understand that these relationships between conscience and the world are dialectic" (p. 25). For Freire, the significance of language lay in its connection to reading, to its serving as the medium through which people could find meaning in the world around them. Just as Fink (2004) attempts to read Lacan "to the letter" to interpret Lacan through the "word," so does Freire use the "word" as a figurative and literal representation of the world. In both instances, Fink and Freire imply that the "word" holds complex meaning, represents much more than a simple array of letter arrangements, and translates between us and the writer.

Equally important, Freire (1998a & 1998b) connects words to conscience, or "right thinking." To speak towards a pedagogy of liberation demands an attunement to justice and honesty. He clearly stipulates, "Whoever is engaged in 'right thinking' knows only too well that words not given body (made flesh) have little or no value. Right thinking is right doing" (p.39). In this way, Freire suggests that libratory thinking will produce a corresponding libratory action. To be a libratory educator is to speak a language of freedom that inspires political agency. He goes on to add,

> In this sense, to teach right thinking is not something that is simply spoken of or an experience that is merely described. But something that is done and lived while it is being spoken of, as if the doing and living of it constituted a kind of irrefutable witness of its truth. To think correctly implies the existence of subjects whose thinking is mediated by objects that provoke and modify the thinking subject. Thinking correctly is, in other words, not an isolated act or something to draw near in isolation but an act of communication (p. 42).

Because "right thinking" imbues "right action," communication exists in the space between thought and agency. And, in this communication, the body translates thought and creates an action indicative of the thought(s). Here again, discourse is important. For Freire, however, discourse must be an embodied discourse; if it is to be a transformative discourse which moves us towards liberation, it must manifest itself in action(s). Discourse without such action is normative, unable to interrupt and disturb the dominant discourses of those in power.

To continue exploring Lacan's relationship to language and cultural studies, I suggest that a re-positioning of Lacan beside literacy would push us to broaden tradition definitions of literacy; if we infuse literacy with Lacan's fascination with spoken language and Freire's notion of reading the word/world, then we can reinterpret literacy. Literacy is about more than reading words; it is about reading oneself, others, and the world. It is about coming to understand the relationship between "I," "Us," and "There." Shannon and Crawford (1998) frame it best when they say, "Our second assumption is that literacy can help citizens to take measure of their lives and the society and to ask, 'Why are things the way they are?' This seemingly innocent question is both a weapon and a tool" (p. 245). Literacy is political. It is a way of reading one's world, coming to identify oppression and privilege, and taking steps to eliminate inequities.

Literacy also reflects a complicated and continuous blending of thinking, speaking, acting, reflecting, and assessing. To "read the word/world" and "act right, " we must be vigilant in our thinking, courageous in our speaking, passionate in our acting, persistent in our reflecting, and careful in our assessing. Though I do not wish to limit literacy to these particular terms, I use them to capture the complexity in maintaining the "Borromean" knot so to speak. Without either of these components, literacy cannot be libratory. Together, thinking, speaking, acting, reflecting, and assessing, create the critical capacity to distance ourselves from the systems, structures, and people we need to study. Freire (1998b) describes this distancing when he gives an example of two participants in a literacy training program; the participants were from Porto Mont. One day, they observed the village from a window and exclaimed, "Yeah, this is what Porto Mont is like, and we didn't even know it!" Freire goes on to say,

> Up until that point, their 'reading' of that locale, of their private world, a reading made extremely close to the 'text,' which was the context of the village, had prevented them from *seeing* Porto Mont as it was. . . *Immersed* in the reality of their small world, they were unable to *see* it. By taking some distance, they *emerged* and were thus able to see it as they never had before (p. 21).

In this context, literacy enables the villagers to see their world, to interpret it, to re-examine it. In the process, they begin to see what had previously been invisible, to understand what had previously been undefined. No longer "in the middle," they can distinguish between different truths of the village – the truth they had known before and the truth they witness now. For them, literacy brings clarity but, in this clarity, they observe and experience contradiction. They must now decide which reality to embrace and which to contest.

Finally, I wish to return to one of the premises of this book – the notion of democratic education. Democratic education is libratory education, education grounded in issues of justice, care, and social agency and also intricately connected to the exercise of power in classrooms. In a democratic classroom, different languages are valued and embraced. Noted critic Lisa Delpit has spent much of her career discussing the relationships between language, education, and power. In the article, "The silenced dialogue: Power and pedagogy in educating other people's children," she responds to the following quote, "Children have the right to their own language, their own culture. We must fight cultural hegemony and fight the system by insisting that children be allowed to express themselves in their own language style" (2003/1996, p. 158). Delpit understands language as a medium of culture. It creates us as social beings bound together in various collectivities, but it also can be manipulated by us, refashioned in unpredictable ways.

Current trends in U.S. public education (and in our increasingly hostile immigration policies) make it more and more difficult for teachers to embrace children's alternative languages. With funding for bilingual education programs cut and ESL (English and a Second Language) programs in place, immigrant students are pushed to learn English more quickly and, as a consequence, they are "losing" their native languages. Portes (2005) documents this trend by saying,

> In no other country, among 35 nations compared in a detailed study by sociologist Stanley Lieberson and his colleagues, did foreign languages fade as swiftly as in the United States. Linguists such as Joshua Fisherman and Calvin Veltman have documented how this takes process takes place. First-generation immigrants learn as much English as they can, but continue to speak their mother tongue at home. The second generation grows up speaking the mother tongue at home, but English at school and at work. By the third generation, English becomes the home language and the transition to monolinguilism is completed (p. 212).

Portes goes on to suggest that there is an acceptance in the United States of foreign languages learned at elite institutions, but a rejection of foreign languages transported across the border by immigrating people. The distinction is one to note because it reflects a certain elitism, a caveat in the dominant discourse that needs unraveling. How can foreign language be esteemed in one setting and completely devalued in the next?

Equally important, teachers are often unwilling to embrace various dialects spoken by students. When in the 1990's, the Oakland district in California attempted to provide professional development workshops for its teachers to help them understand Ebonics (or Black English Vernacular), the public outcry (from some black constituents as well) was enormous. Although the district had no intention of teaching in Ebonics, people expressed concern that children would never learn "standard English" if they were allowed to speak in dialect. This debate exemplified our devaluation of language; for people who value and understand multilingualism, children's capacity to learn different languages seems self evident. They can and do learn to code switch, to change languages in different contexts and/or situations.

As teachers, we are obligated to understand our students, to create spaces where they can express themselves and be valued as integral participants in the educative process. To do so requires that we become as fascinated with language as Lacan was. We must attune ourselves to the spoken and written word; help our students understand that literacy encompasses both and that literacy is an exercise of power.

In a sense, we are like psychoanalysts, for whom speech is the link towards the unconscious. Through studying a patient's speech, psychoanalysts hear/see/ experience the patient's symptoms and these symptoms act as metaphors for unconscious thought. In a similar vein, we must recognize the interruptions in children's speech; we must look for the silences that may indicate/create false discourse. And, in those interruptions and silences, we may begin to understand who our students really are.

NOTES

---

[1] Campbell (2004) also gives an example of the different products of discourse. The discourse of the Master produces jouissance, left-over meaning while the discourse of the Analyst produces the master signifier which represents the subject (p. 51).

CHAPTER 4

LACAN AS CLINICAL PRACTIONER

In his quest to uncover the unconscious, Lacan explored the unknown with a particular kind of hesitant certainty; even though the unconscious was uncharted territory, he presumed that psychoanalytic process could reach its depths. He understood his role as that of an explorer who charted the destination, but who also expected deviations in the journey. And though he realized that each individual's experience of the journey could be different, he hoped that each experience could contribute specific information about the journey (psychoanalytic process) and the destination (the unconscious). As a student of process, the psychoanalyst learned the skills and methods necessary to navigate the unexplored and suppressed; s/he could explain the unexplainable. And just as an explorer would take copious notes, so would a psychoanalyst record her/his observations and interpretations of the journey. Only in this way would s/he ever discover how to return to the unconscious, to reach it as it shifts or retreats.

Similar to the explorer, the psychoanalyst wields significant power. S/he can identify the destination and chart the journey — tell us when we have reached the unconscious and what it is saying to us (or of us). For the psychoanalyst, identification is synonymous with interpretation; as the explorer would identify the "native population" and "explain" their actions and ideologies, so might the psychoanalyst identify the subject of the unconscious and "explain" us to ourselves. S/he can potentially tell us more about ourselves than we wish to admit or are able to acknowledge. The psychoanalyst, therefore, works in and from a precarious position; s/he is often revered for having the ability to discover/chart/interpret the unconscious, but s/he is simultaneously feared for having the extraordinary ability to bring to conscious thought our most avoided desires.

Over the course of his career, Lacan would speak of the role of the psychoanalyst and processes of psychoanalysis. Consistently, he would argue that the psychoanalyst's job was to read, not to fix or correct. In an interview conducted in 1957, he goes into more specific detail about the role of the psychoanalyst and I will quote a portion of the interview here to establish a framework for Lacan as practitioner.

> *Interviewer*: A psychoanalyst is very intimidating. One has the feeling that he could manipulate you as he wishes, that he knows more than you about the motives of your actions.
>
> *Lacan*: Don't exaggerate. Do you think that this effect is exclusive to the psychoanalyst? An economist, for many, is as mysterious as an analyst. In our time, it is the expert who intimidates. With psychology, even when seen as a science, everyone thought they had the insider's track. Now, with psychoanalysis, we have the feeling of having lost that privilege; that the

> analyst could be capable of seeing something quite secret in what appears to you to be quite clear. There you lie naked, uncovered, under a well-informed eye and without knowing what you are showing him.
>
> *Interviewer*: This is a sort of terrorism. One feels violently torn out from oneself.
>
> *Lacan*: Psychoanalysis, in the order of man, has, in fact, all the subversive and scandalous features that the Copernican de-centering had in the cosmic order: the earth, that place inhabited by man, is no longer the center of the universe! Well! Psychoanalysis announces that you are no longer the center of yourself, since there is another subject within you, the Unconscious. . .An analyst must not be seen as a 'soul engineer'; he's not a physician, he does not proceed by establishing cause-effect relations; his science is a reading, it's a reading of sense. This is why, undoubtedly, without knowing exactly what is hidden behind his office's door, he is commonly considered as a sorcerer, an even greater one that the others.[1]

To better understand Lacan's belief that psychoanalysts were viewed as experts, we must remember the historical context of France during the 1950's. Although France had gone through a considerable rebuilding and governmental restructuring process after World War II ended in 1945, by the 1950's the country was struggling to maintain control over its colonies in Africa and Asia. Between 1946 and 1954, Indochina fought to gain its independence and between 1954 and 1958 Algeria followed suit. By 1958, France had adopted the constitution of the Fifth republic and strengthened the power of the executive branch. When Lacan was interviewed in 1957, France was a nation in turmoil, trying to recover the prestige and international dominance it had formerly enjoyed. When he speaks of the authority of experts, he is, in fact, implicating a much larger issue for the nation. Those in positions of power, particularly those in political positions, have come to metaphorically represent the nation's struggle with leadership and authority; the people of France desperately need to believe in their leaders—their experts at a time when their international dominance was being challenged and questioned.

If we consider this metaphor in a larger sense, Lacan's comparison of the psychoanalyst's role to that of the Copernican revolution is important. Just as France's preeminence has been forestalled (the nation is no longer the center of the universe), so does the psychoanalyst de-center the individual. France is, as a nation and people, trying to uncover its collective unconscious just as the analysand in psychoanalysis is trying to discover the "I" of her/his own unconscious. Both of these journeys/discoveries represent a quest for identity, an attempt to define the nation or oneself with respect to new circumstances or revelations. Both journeys demand an interior struggle, a psychological foray into the unknown (Spillers, 1996).

History, for Lacan, was critical to the study of psychoanalysis. As we discussed in Chapter 1, Lacan studied the history of psychoanalysis and always considered his (and others') theories in historical context. This process was threefold: 1) he studied the evolution of psychoanalysis as a field, 2) he studied this evolution in tandem with local, national, and global development, and 3) he studied the development of other fields of inquiry (such as philosophy and mathematics). Fink (2004) perhaps best captures Lacan's "psychoanalyzing of psychoanalysis" by saying,

> Lacan seems to want to read the history of psychoanalytic theory the way Hegel reads history (in his *Lectures on the Philosophy of History*). Lacan does not do so because he believes analytic history is somehow inexorably tending toward Truth, the way Hegel believes history is pursuing its most perfect course; rather he wants to get out of this true impasse, which is both mental and practical, to which analysis has now come (p. 38).[2]

Lacan's analysis of Freud represents this fascination he had for history because he believed studying the evolution of a theory was a necessary practice when analyzing the content of a theory. To study the theory in isolation, as if the content were somehow divorced from time, would be antithetical to Lacan's spirit of psychoanalysis.

SITUATING THE ANALYST IN PSHCYOANALYSIS

If the subject of study for the psychoanalyst is the unconscious, what does that mean for the process of analysis? It means that, in the process, the psychoanalyst must be aware that s/he is not interacting from the conscious "ego" position, but that s/he must also contend with the subject of the unconscious; this subject affects her/his interpretations just as the subject of the unconscious affects the speaking/being of the patient. In *The Direction of the Treatment and the Principles of its Power*, Lacan refuses to delineate a formula for interpretation. Because the subject of the analyst's unconscious also affects the analytic process, it is impossible to say that a single interpretive method can work for every analyst. So, how does the analyst know is her/his interpretation is "correct?"[3] Lacan explains the process this way,

> To give an example, everyone acknowledges in his own way that to confirm that an interpretation is well founded, it is not the conviction with which it is received by the subject that counts, its well-foundedness instead being gauged by the material that emerges afterward. But psychologizing superstition has such a powerful grip on our minds that people always seek out the phenomenon of well-foundedness in the subject's assent, entirely overlooking the consequences of what Freud says about *Verneinung* [negation] as a form of avowal—to say the least, negation by the subject cannot be treated as equivalent to drawing a blank. That is how theory translates the way in which resistance is engendered in practice. It is also what I am trying to convey when I say that there is no other resistance to analysis than that of the analyst himself (Écrits, 595).

Here, Lacan emphasizes the product that emerges from psychoanalytic process. The analyst cannot merely accept the patient's agreement to the interpretation as proof of the usefulness of the interpretation. Rather, the analyst must also take a close look at the negation—that which the subject questions/denies/resists. If the subject "draws a blank" or can offer no explanation, the analyst must consider that negation is a possible "speaking of the unconscious." We cannot accept that the subject "does not know." It is, instead, that the subject cannot "say." Equally important, Lacan makes note of the resistance of the analyst. What is it that s/he cannot "say?"

Fink (2004) provides further explanation of the resistance of the analyst. Fink notes that Lacan emphasizes the importance of the analyst positioning her/himself in the symbolic realm rather than the imaginary. In doing so, the analyst understands her/his position as within language and not the "Real." According to Fink, when the analyst does not situate her/himself in the Imaginary realm, "The analyst does not want to hear or see certain things or misses them because she is looking for confirmation of her preconceived notion regarding where she is situated in the transference, and she thus essentially resists the process of symbolization" (p. 49). The psychoanalyst must not fall into thinking that it is only the subject that resists analysis/interpretation. Resistance also comes from the analyst who refuses to see her/himself as a subject of analysis (rather than the expert interpreter). In doing so, the analyst is bound to interpret resistance from the subject as an attempt to rival the authority of the analyst. In the realm of the Imaginary, the interpretive process becomes much more personal with the analyst assuming that the patient's resistance is specifically directed at the analyst.

If the analyst remains in the realm of the Symbolic, then s/he can stay attuned to the affective nature of language, the ways in which it gives us emotional understanding and categorizes the world. In this way, the analyst understands that, "the symbol is imminent in affect. Most radically stated, effects are not necessarily the same in all cultures or linguistic groupings; it can be argued that they are not universal, transcultural, or transhistorical (Fink, 2004, p. 52). But, what does this really mean in psychoanalysis? Fink (2004) uses one example of an analysis done by Ernst Kris on a man who believed he had plagiarized. Kris ultimately tells the man that he did not plagiarize, but that he wanted to do so. In his critique of Kris' analysis[4] Lacan maintains that Kris erred in not beginning from a Symbolic position. His interpretation presumed a certain reality; the man did not "really" plagiarize. Lacan argues that in the Symbolic order, plagiarism is not "real." Symbolic property does not exist. According to Lacan, if Kris had begun from this perspective, he would have first questioned "why things at the symbolic level took on such accent, such weight" (Fink, 2004, p. 55/Seminar III, 93 & 80).

It is the analyst who knows in the symbolic order; s/he has learned to distinguish between the imaginary projections of the ego and the world as represented through language. To reach this understanding, the analyst must have, at some point, learned to do so as an analysand (patient) or, if not as analysand, then outside of the analytic experience. Campbell (2004) refers to this question of how the analyst knows as an epistemological problem and says that they "vex Lacan throughout his work, since he must provide an account of the analyst's knowledge in order to legitimate his own practice" (p.43). Put another way, the theoretical problem Lacan faces is that he claims that the analyst understands the world from a different field of knowledge than non-analysts. But, he has a hard time explaining how the analyst comes to this different understanding.

If we say that the analyst was at one point an analysand, one who visited an analyst, then the question becomes, how did the very first analyst come to understand the world beyond the imaginary register? S/he would have had to reach this knowledge outside of the analyst-analysand relationship. Then it becomes possible to speculate that people may come to understand knowledge in the symbolic register without the assistance/guidance of an analyst. And, if this is possible, then we could argue that the analyst position is unnecessary. With either explanation, Lacan faces a theoretical problem. In the first, it is the problem of transition; the analyst was once an analysand. In the second instance, the problem is one of legitimization of the field. If it is possible to reach an understanding of the distinction between imaginary and symbolic knowledge without an analyst, then why do we need them (or the field itself)?

Indeed, we must wonder how and when the analyst comes to understand her/his ego as the projector of false consciousness and the subject of the unconscious as the primary motivator. How and when does the analyst analyze her/himself? Lacan addresses this question using a quote from Sandor Ferenczi's article on psychoanalytic elasticity,

> I should like to mention, as a problem that has not been considered, that of the metapsychology of the analyst's mental processes during analysis. His cathexes oscillate between identification (analytic object-love) on the one hand and self control or intellectual activity on the other. During the long day's work he can never allow himself the pleasure of giving his narcissism and egoism free play in reality, and he can give free play to them in his fantasy only for brief moments. A strain of this kind scarcely occurs otherwise in life, and I do not doubt that sooner or later it will call for the creation of a special hygiene for the analyst (Écrits, 340).

What is perhaps most striking about this quote is that, in referring to it, Lacan highlights the analyst's struggle with narcissism and egoism as a continuous one, one that s/he must endure during psychoanalytic sessions. There is a persistent tension between the analyst's subject identification and that of the patient. And because the analyst must assume the role of analyst (interpreter), s/he must maintain a certain amount of composure; s/he must minimize the affects of this tension in the psychoanalytic process and focus on the patient's narrative. This process is thus a demanding one for the psychoanalyst, one that Ferenczi suggests will necessitate a particular kind of treatment for psychoanalysts. After all, who shall analyze the analyst?

TO CURE OR NOT TO CURE: THAT IS THE QUESTION

In his talk entitled "Variations on the standard treatment," Lacan reiterates his belief that psychoanalysis is not a means towards a definitive end. It is not a journey towards a predetermined cure. For this reason, Lacan resists using terminology similar to that used in the medical profession, "improved," "much improved," or "cured." He specifically says of the psychoanalyst,

> While he thus views cure as an added benefit [*la guérison comme benefice de sucroît*] of psychoanalytic treatment, he is wary of any misuse of the desire to cure. This is so ingrained in him that, when an innovation in technique is based upon this desire, he worries deep inside and even reacts inside the analytic group by raising the automatic question 'Is that still psychoanalysis?' (Écrits, 324-325).

Lacan refutes the belief that "to cure" is the goal of psychoanalysis but does not reject the idea that it would be a good by-product of the process. He goes on, in this same seminar, to reject the idea that psychoanalysis can be reduced to a series of simple, reproducible steps. Lacan acknowledges the contradiction inherent in theoretical and practical psychoanalysis. How can we theorize about the importance of psychoanalysis but not have a clear process for its therapeutic application?

Lacan refers to this potential problem by saying, "This paradox is clearly introduced by what all analytic writers express, the most authorized affirming it no less than the others, regarding analysis' therapeutic criteria—namely, that the more stridently we demand a theoretical reference the more these criteria vanish. This is a matter of serious concern, when theory is alleged to give treatment its status" (Écrits, 325). Citing a study done by Edward Glover, in which he sent a questionnaire to twenty-nine psychoanalysts in Great Britain, Lacan notes that there was very little agreement among the respondents regarding standard therapeutic practice. Lacan found the external criticism of psychoanalysis troubling, to say the least. How could psychoanalysis claim a standard treatment when the subject of treatment was the unconscious and the unconscious was/is so unpredictable? In fact, Lacan felt that to ascribe to a predetermined set of therapeutic processes would eliminate the analyst's creativity; it would stifle her/his ability to develop new or varied techniques.

But if the analyst's primary function is not to cure the patient, then what is her/his function? Again, in his seminar, "Variations on the standard treatment," Lacan offers a partial answer. He believes that the analyst's position comes imbued with a set of societal expectations. He says, "A psychoanalysis, whether standard or not, is the treatment one expects from a psychoanalyst" (Écrits, 329). He goes on to add, "Hence the analyst retains complete responsibility, in the weighty sense that I have just defined on the basis of his position as a listener. An ambiguity that is direct, since it is at his own discretion as an interpreter, turns into a secret summons that he cannot dismiss even by remaining silent" (Écrits, 331). It is the anlyst's responsibility to assume the role of analyst, to understand that s/he is expected to understand/interpret. But, Lacan goes even further by emphasizing the ambiguity in the term "analyze." He comments,

> The vague term 'analyzing' all too often makes up for the imprecision that keeps them from using 'interpreting,' because it has not been updated. This is an effect of the notion of the avoidance at work in the practitioner's thinking. The false consistency of the notion of countertransference, its stylishness, and

> the fanfare it fosters can be explained by the fact that it serves as an alibi: the analyst thereby avoids considering the action that it is incumbent upon him to take in the production of truth (Écrits, 331-332).

Although Lacan resists articulating a "standard" treatment, he also understands that some psychoanalysts take this resistance as a reason to not offer any solid interpretations; they are unwilling to offer any specific thoughts regarding the patient's dilemma(s). Lacan takes them to task for not doing what it is they are supposed to do—to interpret. Accepting the ambiguity inherent in psychoanalytic treatment does not give license to psychoanalysts' renouncing of their responsibilities as psychoanalysts.

Lacan embraced the inherently creative nature of psychoanalysis because it, in essence, gave him free reign to restructure the practice of psychoanalysis. Because he believed that the psychoanalyst's primary function was to "read" the subject, he recognized that each psychoanalytic session would be unique and that there could be no universally applied standard treatment. His beliefs led him to deviate from the standard practice of holding one hour psychoanalytic sessions at specific times.

Though Lacan was criticized, at times for being a charlatan, he would always emphasize the psychoanalytic experience; one could not establish predetermined times for the speaking of the unconscious. The unconscious was unpredictable and, therefore, analysts must be unorthodox in their practice. Lacan would hold sessions whenever and wherever the need arose and would, consequently, draw intense criticism from those who did not believe "true" psychoanalysis could occur in places like taxicabs.

THE RELATIONSHIP BETWEEN ANALYST AND ANALYSAND

Unorthodox he was and unlike many of his contemporaries, he did not seek to fulfill the patient's need for identification or the need to position themselves in direct relationship to the being of the analyst. Instead, he sought to push patients away from their natural tendency to rely on the analyst's confirmation/interpretation. For Lacan, this was paramount in psychoanalysis. Analysts must steer patients away from establishing an identity contingent upon the analyst's position as authority figure. Fink (2004) best explains this dilemma by saying,

> A number of Lacan's contemporaries formulated the explicit goal of trying to bring about identification between the analysand and the analyst, which, according to Lacan, involves 'reduc[ing] their patient's desires to demands which simplifies the task of converting them into the analyst's own demands' (E 626). This identification satisfies the analyst's demand for being, the analysand's 'passions for being' (E 627); I know who and what I am because the analyst (as Other) tells me who and what I am . . . Lacan, rather than seeking to satisfy the patient's passion for being which *can* be satisfied through identification—tries to get the analysand to encounter the *manqué-à-être* (lack of being, failure to be, want-to-be) (p. 37).

Lacan's position required analysts to work from a subject position other than the ego. If they did not, the narcissistic nature of the ego would allow the analyst to accept the patient's identification with him or her. The analyst would relish in the self importance gained by such reliance of the patient on his or her interpretation and, in doing so, would allow the patient to achieve a sort of false consciousness.

Fink (2004) discusses Lacan's interpretation of the analytical process as a bridge game. In this game there are four players who each holds a set of cards and these cards represent different ways for each player to interact in the game. Of course, neither player knows what the other holds in his or hand nd the game proceeds with each player trying to outwit the other. As Fink says,

> There are thus always four different players in the analytic game, which Lacan likens here to a game of bridge. . . The analyst has an ego partner, the dummy (or Other as language), and the analysand as ego has a partner too, his unconscious, whose hand is unknown. The analyst's goal is to get the analysand as ego to guess his own partner's hand—that is to devine what is unconscious in himself (p. 5).

Lacan himself discusses the role of the analyst at length in "The direction of the treatment and the principles of its power." He even goes so far as to sarcastically query, ". . . just think of the highmindedness we display when we show that we ourselves are made up of the same clay as those we shape!" (Écrits, 585). Here, Lacan points to fallibility of the analyst—s/he has a dummy partner to interpret just as the analysand has an unconscious to interpret. There is no given script for the analyst to follow; in fact, the analyst must be prepared to interpret language differently in different contexts. Patient's X and Y, for example, may use the same words, but convey entirely different meaning. The analyst may put forth the same statement to Patient's X and Y, but they may interpret that statement in entirely contradictory ways. In his sarcasm, Lacan recognizes the vulnerability of the analyst's position; s/he is not omniscient.

THE CLINICAL PRACTIONER AND EDUCATION

Since Lacan believed so intensely that the analyst must remain cognizant of her/his position in the analytic relationship and in language, he likened the analyst to an educator who, to remain an excellent teacher, must continue to learn. As an educator of and with the psychological, the analyst understands that identity springs forth from intersecting variables (time, circumstance, geographic and social location, etc.). With such an understanding of identity, the analyst must work from a place of uncertainty; with identity contingent upon so many changing variables, the analyst's only certainty is that the unconscious is unknown. What does it mean for the analyst when the subject of her/his work is and always will be the unknown and the unpredictable? At the very least, this suggests that analysts must continue to learn, to experience different contexts so that this learning and these experiences may help in later interpretations.

In much of his work, Lacan critiques analysts who have fallen into the procedural trap, analysts who believe that a step by step method will lead to some "real" interpretation of the patient's dilemma(s). To do so not only limits the interpretive possibilities of the analysis, it also limits the analyst's interpretation to an individual discussion rather than a more comprehensive analysis inclusive of other relational factors. To forego this problem, Lacan suggests that analysts "would do better to take his hearings from his want-to-be than from his being" (Écrits, 589). He goes on to lament (at some length) the problems with analysts who presume a definitive ego posture,

> For contemporary psychoanalysts, this relationship to reality is self-evident. They gauge the patient's defections from it using the authoritarian principle that has been employed by educators since time immemorial. They simply rely on training psychoanalysts to ensure its maintenance at as sufficient rate among analysts, about whom one can't help feeling that, in facing the problems of humanity that are addressed to them, their views are sometimes a bit parochial. This is merely to push the problem back to an individual level. And it is hardly reassuring—when they describe the procedure of analysis as the reduction in the subject of deviations, attributed to his transferences and resistances, but mapped in relation to reality—to hear them gush about the 'perfectly simple situation' that is provided by analysis as a means of assessing those deviations. Come now! The educator is hardly ready to be educated if he can judge so superficially an experience that he, too, must nevertheless have undergone (Écrits, 590).

Here, Lacan's lamentation about the interpretive ability of some psychoanalysts mirrors my own frustration with the "standardization" of the curriculum in education. Lacan notes that the standardization of psychoanalysis leads to an emphasis on the subject's deviations and a presumption that the role of psychoanalysis is to eliminate those deviations. With the standardization of the curriculum in U.S. schools, we are grappling with a similar situation. Students are viewed as test scores needing to be improved and are scrutinized for any deviant behaviors which may be contributing to the low test score. Teachers, particularly those in "low performing schools" (schools which most often have proportionally more African American and Latino children), are inundated with prepackaged curricular materials which (according to some) eliminate the opportunity for deviant behavior and teach children how to pass particular tests[5]

If we compare the educator/teacher to the clinical practitioner, there are some distinct differences, differences that might account for high teacher turnover rates and disillusionment with the profession. I think it might be useful here to begin with an example, one taken from my own experiences as a high school teacher in North Carolina. I was in my fourth year of teaching. One day, while sitting in a faculty meeting (unwillingly, of course…I had papers to grade, students to tutor—no time for a faculty meeting), I made a decision to leave teaching in K-12 public schools. Our principal began the meeting with the usual mundane announcements but then, towards the end of the meeting, announced a change in policy regarding teacher use of planning period time[6] Typically, teachers used this time to grade papers, made copies, make lesson plans, or collaborate with other teachers. Teachers whose planning period coincided with lunch time would sometimes go out for lunch. At this particular faculty meeting, however, our principal chastised faculty for going out to lunch and said, "If you want to be treated like professionals, you have to act like professionals." At the moment, I snapped out of my apathetic stupor and thought, "Since when can professionals *not* go out to lunch?" And, I wanted to scream, "So what should we do, just place our orders through the office staff (administrators included)?—many of them ordered lunch on a daily basis and/or left campus to pick up lunch. I was furious but silent.

This became a moment of clarity for me. I realized that, somehow, by becoming a public school teacher, I had psychologically regressed—become obedient to a fault and lost the will to openly rebel. Instead, I (like many of my other colleagues), protested amongst ourselves but settled for deafening silence in faculty meetings; I was more interested in shortening the length of the meeting than in beginning a prolonged debate, a debate that I was sure would be futile. Though I was not one of the accused when my principal demanded that faculty cease going off campus for lunch, I realized that I was not a professional; I was not, as a teacher, considered capable of managing my own time, making independent curricular decisions, or free to express any kind of individual agency (unless, of course, it resulted in higher test scores). The lunch issue was just one of a whole host of other insults on our integrity and I began to plan my escape.

I relate this incident for several reasons, 1) I believe that thousands of "little" incidences or seemingly innocuous ones like this one illustrate teachers being treated as dependent and incompetent beings, 2) As a result, teacher time is micro-managed, pre-determined, and compartmentalized, 3) Teachers are effectively de-professionalized.[7] To be a teacher then differs vastly from being a clinical practitioner. The standardization of the profession, though intended to ensure the delivery of a quality education to all children, also eliminates opportunities for teacher creativity and spontaneity. While clinical practitioners, in Lacanian terms, should be valued for their authority, creativity, and spontaneity, teachers are struggling to maintain these same attributes despite enormous structural pressure to "do everything the same" (e.g. teach the same content, in the same way, and in the same amount of time).

Lacan's recognition that few of his contemporaries practiced using exactly the same standards is relevant for those of us teaching today. For him, each patient was distinct, motivated by the unknown of the unconscious. To reach that unconscious demanded strategies specific to the patient; it required an attunement to her/his speech, silence, and interruptions. With a complete standardization of the curriculum, there is little room for teachers to attune themselves to individual students' speech, silences, and interruptions. Rather, teachers must herd students along through state mandated content with few pauses for "irrelevant" interruptions. Of the many teachers I have talked with, none have expressed a love for the increasing standardization of the curriculum and few believe they have the capacity to halt the current high stakes testing fervor. Instead, they continue to teach, hoping to inspire those creative moments in children that keep them interested in school.

The role of the teacher in this environment seems self evident—to deliver the content as prescribed by the state. But, there still exists a much larger mandate for schools and teachers. When I entered teaching, I hoped that I would arouse in children a passion for learning; I hoped that I would be able to cultivate their own particular talents and help them to appreciate the value of those talents. But, I quickly learned that the school is a politically contested site, one where competing interests collide and various policy makers favor curricular programs that can reach the "majority" of children. To create and embrace a curricular program that would individually tailor content to each child seems beyond the reach/understanding of those who tell us what to teach. Spring (2006) points out that public education remains a primary concern of the Republican, Democrat, and Green parties, but only the Green party's 2004 platform put forth an educational agenda which emphasized education for the betterment of the community. Both the Republican and Democratic parties directly tied the purpose of public education to creating an improved workforce. Equally important, Spring emphasizes the fact that political officials are responsible for directing, maintaining, and revising school policies.

> Public schools exist to serve public goals. The public goals of schooling are determined by elected representatives in local, state, and federal governments. U.S. public schools were established to reduce political and social unrest by teaching future citizens a common set of political values and patriotism; to reduce social tensions by promising equality of opportunity; to decrease crime by teaching morality; and to eradicate poverty by stimulating economic growth. Twentieth- and twenty-first-century concerns with urbanization, industrialization, racial and cultural harmony, juvenile crime, nutritional health, epidemic diseases and globalization add to these early goals (p. 9).

If these have all become the goal of public education, then what has become the role of the teacher? Spring goes on to question,

> Can teachers actually integrate character education into their teaching as recommended by No Child Left Behind? Can teachers of reading, writing, arithmetic, English, history, science, and other school subjects actually impart knowledge and values that will reduce crime, promote racial and economic harmony, increase employment opportunities, stabilize the political system, and prepare for globalization (p. 10)?

Public schools are implicitly grounded in one of the founding principles of U.S. government, "majority rules, minority rights." We govern by consent of the majority and hope that the majority continues to protect and acknowledge the rights of those who do not share the same views. In civic life and in schools, we have yet to effectively protect the rights of the minority. Much of our confusion stems from our inability to clearly say that some rights are not worth protecting. Some, for example, somehow believe that to protect freedom of speech, we must protect the rights of hate groups. Until we can clearly define whose or what rights are fundamental, we will have a serious problem in public schools. Schools and teachers must have a moral mission. The question is, how do we find that mission with so many competing interests at stake?

To reconsider curriculum in a moral sense and a Lacanian context requires a reconsideration of what we mean when we say "public education." Public education does not mean that we ignore the individual; to do so would leave us with a curriculum that fails to connect with many students. I believe this is precisely what we have done; we have taken the concept of "public" to give license to the ignoring of students' individual needs. And we expect them to embrace this education because it will afford them greater economic opportunity later in life. In the interim, we have forgotten that the present and presence are still important. Many of us are not living in cultural or economic harmony in the present nor do we know what it means to be fully present in the now. To teach in a Lacanian context is to teach in the unknown. To hear and translate the speaking unconscious is indeed a moral act; it is so precisely because it facilitates an individual's understanding of her/himself. It brings us closer to being an integrated subject, cognizant of the self as determined by that which we cannot so easily identify.

To teach from a moral position in an institution purportedly dedicated to the public good is not impossible. Contrary to popular belief, there are some issues which are universally subjects of moral concern, issues which have very real personal meaning and public ramifications. Purpel (1999) best captures this moral positioning by responding to the 1998 presidential campaign,

> There was virtually no mention of poverty or racism; no reference to hunger and homelessness; no sense of outrage at unnecessary human suffering. Instead of debate on the plight of the homeless, there were ploys to attract soccer moms; the war on poverty had been replaced by a crusade for middle-class tax relief . . . While politicians spin, educators test, critics reflect, and theorists parse, there are people eating dog food, teenagers turning tricks, children dealing in drugs, and families living in boxes. I say all this because I believe that it is intolerable that there be any educational discourse without continuous reference to the presence of pain and suffering that is rooted in human greed, irresponsibility, and callousness (as cited in Shapiro and Purpel, 2005, p. 350).

To teach from a moral position is to recognize the pain and suffering that inflicts us in personal and communal ways. In the U.S. and particularly in public schools, we live with the myth of meritocracy—the belief that any individual who works hard enough can succeed. This is a myth because it simply is not true, it is not universally applicable. Many people work hard everyday but are still unable to pay their bills or purchase the basic necessities of life. Many students do well in school but are unable to attend the college of their choice or to pursue the career of their dreams. But our continued reverence for this myth leads us to presume that suffering is a natural and healthy part of life.

Many of my students in my undergraduate Foundations of Education classes have commented that suffering teaches us to overcome obstacles; it gives us strength and courage. I have to remind them that suffering is a horrific lived experience, not just a means to an end (e.g., "If I overcome suffering, I will be more able to succeed in life"). Because they believe in the myth of meritocracy (which is a fundamental part of the "American dream"), they believe that suffering is an inevitable *and* necessary part of human life. Their responses to suffering thus reflect a poignant de-sensitization. If we are to re-conceive public education from a Lacanian perspective, then we must consider education as fundamentally a sensitizing one. It is and should be a moral endeavor that forces us to teach/live/learn at the intersection of the known and the unknown, the conscious and the unconscious. As such, it is and should be an endeavor that reconnects us to the true "subject" of teaching and learning—the self.

NOTES

[1] From an Interview with Lacan retrieved on October 3, 2005 from http://www.braungardt.com/Psychoanalysis/Lacan-Inteview.htm

[2] Fink cites Lacan's Seminar I, 32/24 as the basis for his interpretation here.

[3] I place correct in quotation marks here because it yields an imprecise understanding of interpretation. It implies that there is one right answer and several wrong ones. In the analytic process, interpretation is useful if it leads to some other meaningful understandings.

[4] See Lacan's Seminars I and III as well as Écrits.

[5] For more specific information on the standardization of U.S. schools, it would be helpful to begin by reading *A nation at risk* report (1983) and the full text of the federal *No Child Left Behind* legislation. Several authors have documented this standardization and its effects. See, Berlak (2005), McNeil (2005), and Sadovnik, Cookson, Jr. and Semel (2001).

[6] I taught at a school with a four period day. Students took four classes per term (August-December and January-May). Teachers had one planning period per term and each period was one and a half hours.

[7] Many other authors have discussed the implications of the de-professionalization of teachers including Anyon (2005), Carlson & Apple (1998), Giroux (1993), McLaren (1993, 1995, & 2003), Kincheloe, Slattery, and Steinberg (2000), Shapiro & Purpel (2005), Spring (2006).

CHAPTER 5

JOUISSANCE — POSTMODERN, POST-STRUCTUTURAL, POST-FORMAL THINKING: IS IT WHATEVER GETS YOU OFF?

In our discussions thus far, we have delved into Lacan's concept of the mirror stage and its relationship to identity development, his work as a teacher and practitioner, and his pursuit of the unconscious. Because we are, ultimately, concerned with Lacan's relevance to our work as educators, we must now push towards further contextualizing his theories with various discourses which shape educational policy today. To do so requires an introduction of one more key concept in Lacanian theory—that of jouissance—and a dialogue between this concept with postmodern, post-structural, and post-formal thinking. In initiating this dialogue, I will provide some common definitions of each concept but will also illustrate the ways in which each is multiply complicated and equally as difficult to singularly define.

Let us begin with Lacan's concept of jouissance. In *Encore: The Seminar of Jacques Lacan Book XX*, Lacan says, "jouissance is what serves no purpose" (1998, 3). By some, it has been translated as "lust" or "enjoyment" but, if we have learned anything of Lacan in the last few chapters, we should realize that Lacanian terminology is never so simple. As Braunstein (2003) notes, the meaning of jouissance is "difficult to translate into English" and "all translators have noted the conceptual loss that is sustained in the use of these terms" (enjoyment and lust) (p. 103). Braunstein goes on to compare desire to jouissance by explaining, "If desire is fundamentally lack, lack in being, jouissance is positivity, it is a 'something' lived by a body when pleasure stops being pleasure. It is a plus, a sensation that is beyond pleasure" (p. 104). While several theorists have equated jouissance to "satisfaction" or "the satisfaction of the drive,"[1] Braunstein reminds us that, for Lacan, jouissance is about more than satisfaction. It is not about satisfying any physical need or desire, but is, instead, about resolving the tension between discourse (as represented by the signifier) and history.

Jouissance, therefore, is not a concept rooted in individual experience; it is, rather, a concept dependent on the Other. If we remember that the "I" for Lacan exists in/through language, then we can understand jouissance as a "sensation beyond pleasure" which is contingent upon the relationship of the self to the Other and history. If we go further and recall that much of Lacanian theory is rooted in his understanding and furthering of Freud's structural theory of the id, ego, and superego, then we can also surmise that jouissance is tied to the relationship between the three. The ego (the projection of self) must mediate between the id, locus of the unconscious, instinctual impulses and the superego, the locus of morality. Thus when Lacan, in Seminar XX says, "Nothing forces anyone to enjoy (*jouir*) except the superego. The superego is the imperative of jouissance — Enjoy!" (p. 3), he is situating jouissance in a particular relationship between the id, ego, and superego. In essence, he tells us that the superego allows us to enjoy the impulses that drive us and, in doing so, jouissance shapes the development of the ego (the representative self).

Fink (2004) attempts to explain Lacan's concept of jouissance further by postulating a divide between language and jouissance. For Fink, Lacan's belief that jouissance is "that which serves no purpose,"[2] suggests that jouissance falls into the realm of the linguistically unexplainable. It is beyond a singular, simplistic definition. But we have a need to name, to categorize, and to interpret. So, how does Fink best describe jouissance? He says, "If language is what makes us different from animals, jouissance is what makes us different from machines" (p. 124). In this way, jouissance gives us the capacity to go beyond the mechanistic, to respond to sensory experiences in meaningful and profound ways. Jouissance, in a sense, allows for life. It is that which gives us the capability to be more than the sum of our parts — it allows for a synergy that is impossible to duplicate with machines.

Finally, when discussing jouissance, we cannot do so without speaking of its erotic implications. These are connected to both the physical act of sex and the language which describes it (for what would one be without the other?). Žižek (2005) describes it best when he says,

> On the one hand we have the closed, ultimately solipsistic circuit of drives that find their satisfaction in idiotic masturbatory (auto-erotic) activity, in the perverse circulating around *objet a* as the object of a drive. On the other hand, there are subjects for whom access to jouissance is much more closely linked to the domain of the Other's discourse, to how they not so much talk as they are talked about: erotic pleasure hinges, for example, on the seductive talk of the lover, on the satisfaction provided by speech itself, not just on the act in its stupidity. Does this contrast not explain the long-observed difference as to how the two sexes relate to cybersex? Men are much more prone to use cyberspace as a masturbatory device for their lone playing, immersed in stupid repetitive pleasure, while women are more prone to participate in chat rooms, using cyberspace for seductive exchanges of speech (pp. 332-33).

As Žižek explains, "true" sex can occur in conversation. And, in this way, jouissance comes into play through language. The act of sex itself, while important, is not necessarily the act which will propel one towards jouissance. It is, instead, the way one talks about the act that gives it meaning and significance. As a result, we experience jouissance in the Symbolic order — it has meaning through language. For this reason, jouissance represents much more than the sensation of pleasure. To know pleasure, one has to describe it, to explain it in some way or to define it as something which it is not. And to describe/explain/define it situates the experience within a larger realm of linguistic understanding. And, it situates it in relationship to other concepts/terms. To know what pleasure is, one must also know what it is not. If we consider this point further, we must acknowledge that all of our definitions are made in relationship — we must have some understanding of other concepts/terms in order to grasp the meaning of the term in question.

POSTMODERNISM

To describe postmodernism, I feel it necessary to begin by defining modernism. Modernism (also equated with positivism), is a way of viewing/understanding the world in which the human experience can be explained through scientific study and inquiry. From a modernist perspective, we need only use proper scientific methodology to reach the "Truth." And, using proper scientific methodology will lead us to unquestionable and verifiable answers. In this way of understanding the world, the human condition is quantifiable — statistics and numbers can explain lived experience. Postmodernism developed in response to modernism; some theorists began to postulate that the human experience was/is not always quantifiable. "Proper" scientific methodology will not always lead us to the "Truth." And, instead, extensive study might lead us to multiple truths. Indeed, the human condition is not so easily explainable, is understood from particular cultural perspectives and as a result, means that knowledge is contextualized.

Jean-François Lyotard (1984), considered the father of postmodernism, argued that the computer age would lead to a particular valuing of "technical" knowledge. As such, any knowledge which could not fit into the modern paradigm would lose its value. I will quote him at some length here,

> The nature of knowledge cannot survive unchanged within this context of general transformation. It can fit into new channels, and become operational, only is learning is translated into quantities of information. We can predict that anything in the constituted body of knowledge that is not translatable in this way will be abandoned and that the direction of new research will be dictated by the possibility of its eventual results being translatable into computer language. The 'producers' and users of knowledge must now, and will have to, possess the means of translating into these languages whatever they want to invent or learn. Research on translating machines is already well advanced. Along with the hegemony of computers comes a certain logic, and therefore a certain set of prescriptions determining which statements are accepted as 'knowledge' statements...Knowledge is and will be produced in order to be sold, it is and will be consumed in order to be valorized in a new production: in both cases, the goal is exchange. Knowledge ceases to be an end in itself, it loses its 'use value' (p. 4)

Lyotard suggests that, with the coming of the computer age, the very definition of what constitutes knowledge will hinge on how it furthers the technological revolution. In this respect, the only kind of knowledge that is valued is technical knowledge—knowledge that is easily quantifiable and verifiable. It is a kind of knowledge contingent upon input and output with little concern for the meaning that occurs in the process of exchange. It is the exchange itself that becomes important and, as such, the only useful knowledge is the kind that facilitates the exchange.

From a postmodern perspective, we are always concerned with meaning. And because the human experience is so vast, we recognize the multiple possibilities inherent in the search for meaning. Meaning is not and cannot be based upon an input/output paradigm. It is not a simple question of measuring the product of an exchange. In our quest for meaning, we look for the immeasurable, the differentiated, and the illusory. Such answers are not variables in an equation with a singular answer. They are, instead, detours along a journey with multiple possible destinations. Equally important, Lyotard calls into question the use of knowledge as a force of production in developing countries. For such nations, knowledge which is considered scientific has the ability to advance production in particular areas (the weapons and pharmaceutical industries are prime examples). Other areas, like the performing arts, are not considered scientific; this type of knowledge is not valued as is technical knowledge, and, as a result, production in this area is not emphasized by those in positions of power.

At this point, we will turn to another theorist who is often labeled postmodern—Michel Foucault. For Foucault, it is actually the notion of counter-modernity which shapes his suggestion that modernity is an attitude rather than an epoch. Counter-modernity demands a constant conversation with the *attitude* of modernity, a persistent unraveling of the metanarratives that determine our understanding of self, history, and reality. Both Foucault and Lyotard believed that we could only understand personal and collective identities in a postmodern sense—neither is stable. Instead, we understand the self as a fiction, an invention which exercises power in relationship. For Foucault (1997), it was this idea of power as an exercise (rather than a possession) which complicates our articulation of oppression and its relationship to knowledge.

If we conceive of power as an exercise rather than a possession, then we must understand it as contextualized, as dependent on the nature of our relationship to others and the world. In this way, we cannot say "I don't have power" or "She has the power" because these statements reflect too simplistic of an understanding of power. Both statements ignore the fact that we wield power differently in different relationships. For example, as a student, you might not wield much power in the classroom (although I would hope that we were all democratic educators who understand the importance of everyone's voice in the classroom). But, once you enter student teaching, your role becomes much more complicated. Technically, you may still be a student, but you are also a teacher. You, therefore, exercise power differently depending on the particular role you need to fulfill at the moment. In essence, we represent multiple identities and each identity enters into relationships with different possibilities for exercising power.

Because postmodernism is a way of viewing the world which embraces the multiplicity of identity, it is also a theory which has various interpretations and articulations across academic disciplines. There is no one way to explain postmodernism, but there are some key common interpretations which tend to cross content areas. As Leicester (2000) says,

> The feature of postmodernism perhaps most frequently mentioned is that it endorses a plurality of perspectives; a plurality of perspectives both in the sense of recognition of the validity of a multiplicity of perspectives or accounts or theories about the 'same' thing, and in the sense of encouraging a way of thinking that is eclectic, drawing on several perspectives, as in the synthesis of elements from more than one cultural tradition, for example. It encourages a blurring or flexibility of boundaries . . .We see here the importance of a concern with language, and of interpretation. There is no one essential meaning to a text; the text is open to a multiplicity of interpretations (p. 74).

Herein lies the connection between postmodernism and Lacanian theory. If we use a postmodern lens to examine Lacanian theory, then we can accept the variations in interpretations of his work. This does not mean that all interpretations are "equal," but it does suggest that all interpretations have a place in the debate. In addition, using a postmodern lens facilitates a more in depth discussion of Lacan's identity theories and his emphasis on the unconscious. We can thus speak of the mirror stage as a complex creation of the contextualized self; it is not the actual emergence of a singular identity but, rather, the construction of a multifaceted singular illusion.

CURRICULUM

Now, if we think for a moment about the relationship between knowledge, power, and identity, we will have to examine the intersections of all three in more detail. Let us begin with the subject of knowledge. In his essay on "The will to knowledge," Foucault (1997) borrows from Nietzsche's description of knowledge. Foucault thus describes knowledge in this way,

> Knowledge is an 'invention' behind which there is something quite distinct from it: an interplay of instincts, impulses, desires, fear, will to appropriation. It is on the stage where they clash that knowledge comes into being. . .it is always servile, dependent, alert to advantage (not to its own but to what might interest the instinct or instincts that dominate it) and if it professes to be a knowledge of the truth, this is because it produces the truth through the action of a primordial and renewed falsification that establishes the distinction between the untrue and the true (p. 14).

Foucault also adds that knowledge is a "series of events" rather than a "permanent faculty." Using his conceptualization, knowledge is more of a process than a fact. It develops as a result of relationship and interactions. And, more important, it is created; it is not universally applicable but, instead, is contingent upon the interests of those who create it.

For educators, it is the false distinction between the untrue and the true that needs to be examined intensely. Foucault suggests that interest determines what we define as knowledge and how we define it as such. Consequently, interests use knowledge as a "mere instrument" and thus knowledge becomes "truth" only when it serves specific purposes or advances the interests of a particular group. We must then ask, "who?" rather than "what?" and "why?" rather than "when?" Asking "who?" and "why?" forces us to associate knowledge with particular interests and motivations. Using this perspective, we must consider curriculum as a set of perspectives rather than a collection of "truths" or "facts." The knowledge that we privilege as curriculum reflects a particular set of interests which convey a particular set of meaning. And this meaning sends implicit messages about what is right and wrong, good and bad, possible and impossible.

Equally important, curriculum (and the knowledge it privileges) sends specific messages about *who* is worthy of study—knowledge thus facilitates the construction of identity, marginality, and difference. Edgerton (1996) refers to Pinar's (1975) curriculum work when discussing the relationship between curriculum and identity. In particular, she grounds her discussion in Pinar's definition of curriculum. Pinar refers to the Latin root of curriculum—currere. Translated, currere means "the running of the course (a race, the course of one's life, etc.), and its study "involves investigation of the nature of the individual experience of the public" (Pinar, 1975, p. 400 & Edgerton, 1996, p. 38). If we are to think of curriculum in this way, we should consider it a journey, one which furthers one's understanding of one's place in the world. Curriculum is, ultimately, about connection, relationship, and learning.

To enact this particular definition of curriculum, we must engage in some amount of self exploration. Edgerton speaks to the idea of autobiography — a way of "storying" our lives. In constructing narratives of the self, we begin to take an introspective look at the entanglement of the individual and the collective. In doing so, we come to understand how we come to identify marginality and difference as experiences particular to our personal lives. When we selectively choose to write our stories of marginality and difference, Edgerton suggests that we are "choosing to dwell in the margins" (p. 39). She goes on to say,

> A curriculum of marginality is also about excavating excluded stories or storying 'unique outcomes,' in the interest of constructing and performing alternative meanings and ways of being in the world. To the extent the social-communal layer of marginality (discussed further below) is repressed and denied in school curricula, pushed underground in favor of 'happy' and 'safe' reading and writing, the dominant stories that support social neurosis and psychosis (apathy and violence) cannot be challenged (p. 39).

So while educators need to be concerned with curriculum content, they need to do so with particular vigilance of curricula that ignore "controversial" issues. Such curricula, in their complacency, prevent students and teachers from engaging with content which challenges dominant paradigms or modes of thinking. In doing so, we are educating students for conformity rather than rebelliousness. And without both, they can not fully participate in democratic processes which demand that citizens critique and contest.

When considering curriculum and its reflection or construction of marginality and difference, educators must also thoughtfully examine the ways in which curricula negate, erase, or represent particular groups of people. Inevitably, the curriculum chosen identifies certain groups as important and others as less than. Given the limitations of time and space, I do not believe that all groups can be "equally" represented in any given course of study. But, at the very least, groups can be equitably represented — represented with attention to the complexities of difference and the enactment of power in society. This means that we must recognize the celebration of heroes and holidays as inadequate if these are the only ways we discuss people considered "different." It means that we must go beyond the easily identifiable when teaching about people and, instead, grapple with the complicated, complex, and convoluted. Adrienne Rich (1979) best captures the relationship between curriculum, teaching, and identity when she says,

> When those who have the power to name and to socially construct reality choose not to see you or hear you, whether you are a dark-skinned, old, disabled, female, or speak with a different accent or dialect than theirs, when someone with the authority of a teacher, say, describes the world to you and you are not in it, there is a moment of psychic disequilibrium, as if you looked in the mirror and saw nothing (p. 199).

For Rich, the intersection of curriculum, identity, and power is quite clear — those who exercise power construct curriculum and curriculum constructs identity (for the individual and the collective). To teach thus requires a recognition of this intersection and a willingness to deconstruct dominant paradigms which ignore the work/writings/realities of particular groups.

Equally important, educators must understand their role in the curriculum process as more than a transmitter of knowledge — educators are also co-constructors of knowledge. As such, educators mediate between objectivity and subjectivity, between the world of "fact" and "opinion." And while I do not argue that such worlds are distinct entities, I am suggesting that their constant articulation and reiteration makes them "real" and, therefore, separable to us in many ways. We believe that facts are "True" and opinions are, at best, different versions of the truth and, at worst, individual perceptions. And because we believe in such distinctions, we (as educators) may not recognize that our belief in the teacher as "transmitter" of knowledge mirrors Freire's (1970) explanation of banking education. In this role, the teacher simply deposits information in the child's brain and withdraws that information at a specified time. Freire's critique of this type of education is clear. It does not encourage critical thinking nor does it support praxis—reflective thought and action. When students are only expected to regurgitate knowledge, they spend little time reflecting on how that knowledge might change reality or how that knowledge might be critiqued.

For an educator to accept and understand her/his role as co-constructor of curriculum, s/he must understand the various ways s/he exercise power in the learning process. To further explore this role, let us go back to Foucault's (1997) articulation of power. Simply put, he argued that power was an exercise which occurred because of and in relationship. But, he went on to describe a more complex relationship between knowledge and power and the subject and truth. This explanation is worth reiterating here in our discussion of curriculum. Foucault discusses these concepts as pairs (knowledge and power; the subject and truth) yet he does not imagine them as interchangeable in any way. Instead, he says,

> As I said when we started, I have always been interested in the problem of the relationship between subject and truth. I mean, how does the subject fit into the game of truth? The first problem I examined was why madness was problematized, starting at a certain time and following certain processes, as an illness falling under a certain model of medicine. How was the mad subject placed in this game of truth by a medical model or a knowledge? And it was while working on this analysis that I realized that, contrary to what was rather common practice at that time (around the early sixties), this phenomenon could not be properly accounted for simply by talking about ideology. In fact, there were practices—essentially the widespread use of incarceration which had been developed starting at the beginning of the seventeenth century, and had been the condition for the insertion of the mad subject in this type of truth game—that sent me back to the problem of institutions of power much more than the problem of ideology (pp. 289-90).

He then goes on to add that he does not view the relationship between knowledge and power as the fundamental question, but as "an instrument that makes it possible to analyze the problem of the relationship between subject and truth in what seems to me the most precise way" (p. 290). For Foucault, there exists a dependency in the relationship between the pairs — knowledge and power; subject and truth — which insinuates that any analysis must consider both pairs in simultaneity. In other words, we must use the relationship between knowledge and power as a sort of mediator in our discussions of the relationship between subject and truth.

It is precisely this relationship between subject and truth; knowledge and power which has significant implications in and for Lacanian theory. Since Lacan believed that the subject was constituted through language, we can infer that truth is bound by language and, therefore, dependent on its nuances as well as its flux. Similarly, knowledge is a product of language and is born of the relationship between words. For Lacan, knowledge comes from the unconscious and, thereby, represents the tension between what we believe we "know" and that which we do not or can not access, acknowledge, or admit. To analyze the intersection (parallels or divergences) of subject and truth; knowledge and power, I rely on Campbell's (2004) feminist and Lacanian interpretations. She argues that,

> (1) The knowing subject is not external to social relations but is constituted by them;
>
> (2) Political values are not excluded from knowledge but are epistemologically significant;
>
> (3) Knowledge is not an objective mirror of the external world, as social practices construct it (p. 14).

Ultimately, she reiterates the idea that "knowing subjects produce knowledges" (p. 14). And, she maintains that Lacan perceived there to be no objective distance between the truth and language. She sums up this belief quite nicely by saying, "In the Lacanian model of knowledge, there is no possibility of a neutral representation of reality, precisely because to describe an object involves representing it in language" (p. 35). To further this point, she quotes Lacan by saying, "there is no such thing as a metalanguage. . . no language able to say the truth about the truth since truth is grounded in the fact that it speaks, and that it has no other means with which to do so" (*Écrits*, 1965, 867-868; Campbell, 2004, p. 35). It is impossible for us to escape, to claim some consistently stable place outside of language; we, as subjects, both produce and reproduce language. Thus, we produce and reproduce knowledge. And this productive process takes place within constructed networks of power that are also constituted by and within language.

POST-STRUCTURALISM

And so we come back to language as well as the title for this chapter. Now that we have a context and understanding of postmodernism, let us discuss post-structuralism. Although we have reviewed post-structuralism briefly in previous chapters, a more detailed explanation is necessary to discuss post-structuralism in parallel to postmodernism and, later, post-formalism. Of course, to understand post-structuralism, we must first begin with structuralism. So, let us begin. Structuralism is a linguistic theory grounded in the work of Swiss linguist de Sausurre. Sausurre believed that to understand language, one must study it as a formal system. Olssen (2003) sums up de Sausurre's theory by saying,

> Language formed a system because it belonged to individuals collectively, and constituted a social institution. De Sausurre privileged spoken language and represented the system as made up of sounds and as having meaning. Hence, the sign is a set of sounds (a 'signifier') which has a meaning (a 'signified'). The signified was not the referent of the object, however, but rather the concept, or sense, which the sign expressed. Signs were 'arbitrary', in de Sausurre's view, in that there was no necessary relation between a sign and its referent. Rather, signs were defined in relation to other signs. What characterizes a language then is a *system of differences*, and the kinds of differences that a language embodies are central to the way that objects in reality are classified and categorized as the basis of a common understanding in the society (p. 190).

The implications of de Sausurre's work are important. Using his theory, we can infer that the meaning of language comes through in the relationship between words. A word by itself has no meaning. Language can thus be understood as a "functional system to be understood in terms of its aim (communication)" (p. 190). If we return to Lacan's suggestion that the subject is constituted in and through language, then we can see how he used the basic tenets of structuralism to relate identity to the unconscious — since the unconscious is structured like a language, then we must study it as such a structure to gain some understanding of the self or subject.

Perhaps what is most intriguing about structuralism is its refutation of causality. Foucault, who was occasionally linked to structuralism (though he denied being one), embraced this refutation and argued that, in studying language as a structure, we should be concerned with identifying the multiple relationships between words/concepts. Instead of being examined in linear fashion, identity (individual and collective) can be analyzed as a whole composed of constituent parts which venture in multiple directions. It is this emphasis on the whole which bothers Foucault and moves him towards a post-structuralist orientation. He was unwilling to concede that understanding the structure would inevitably lead one to understand the particular parts. And, he did not believe structuralism could account for what preceded language — there is a system of meaning in place which contextualizes language. For Foucault, this system was power. Indeed, power relationships imbue meaning in language and facilitate the applicability of that meaning to people's everyday lives.

Foucault was particularly interested in the material elements of power relationships, the elements of coercive force which create meaning. There is a distinct relationship between language and the material but the material constructs meaning from its materiality as well and this meaning is not necessarily limited by language. As do other post-structuralists, Foucault is concerned with the meaning created in collective social relationships. In this sense, he and other post-structuralists differ from structuralists in their focus on constituent differences rather than the holistic. Because of this focus on difference, post-structuralists do not (as do structuralists) analyze a text, circumstance, statement, event, etc. as separate from its author. As Peters (2003) argues,

> Structural analysis concentrated on the text as an independent object and not something that was spiritually related to the author. The mistake, however, was twofold. First, to completely remove the text from the author, and the reader for that matter, was to deny any human role in the process. The text becomes a bloodless structural abstraction that is removed from real human interpretation. . .The second 'mistake of structuralism is to leave the leap from phonetics to larger units of analysis unexamined . . . Phonetic rules can be written that have universal linguistic applications and even variations are systematically related to photo-phonetic rules. But assuming that such principles of *langue* can be applied wholesale to actual language use and illuminate the global nature of narrative structure is hubris of the first order (p. 215).

For post-structuralists, there is something *more than* structure. The structure of language, in and of itself, can not explain the whole of any system. And, there is more to communication than language. As we all know, communication hinges upon various emotional and/or psychological implications. Language is about understanding the whole context of communication—the body language, instincts, and affectivities that shape it. Ellis (1994) even argues that thought can exist outside of language and that, for some deaf children, problem solving occurs without language. Problem solving ability hinges more upon interaction than language.

Ultimately, Ellis describes the distinction between structuralists and post-structuralists as one related to the difference between form and meaning. Using the work of post-structuralist Jacques Derrida, Ellis points out that structuralists work with the assumption that there is some commonly understood meaning — a center of understanding. Post-structuralists do not believe in such a center of meaning. For them, such an assumption gives rise to oppressive ideologies which can appear to be politically neutral. Here, I find it necessary to interject a point. In working with public school teachers in the U.S., I have discovered a particular hesitancy from them to tackle "controversial" issues when they teach. For those who do, they articulate an expectation that their jobs may be in jeopardy for doing so. This argument has been particularly poignant when we discuss how to support gay and lesbian children in schools — the vast majority of the teachers I teach believe they would be fired just for mentioning the subject. These teachers view this as a "taboo" subject and, in doing so, fail to realize that gay and lesbian students (or those in families that reflect or support this as a way of being), are not merely controversial subjects. They are, instead, people who represent the communities in which we live and, as such, worthy of discussion. To not discuss them is to ignore them and to ignore them is, in essence, to silence them. If we reconsider the notion that curriculum is about personal journeys, then we realize that the silencing[3] of any student is antithetical to our work as educators.

If we remember that Lacan believed the unconscious was structured like a language, we can impose an interesting post-structuralist interpretation to his work and use that interpretation to elaborate on what public education in the U.S. has become. In suggesting that the unconscious is structured like a language, Lacan operates from a structuralist perspective. But, in situating the subject in the unconscious, Lacan decenters the subject. In doing so, he decenters the meaning that is attached to the conscious subject, the subject situated in what we believe to be conscious thought. For post-structuralists, it is this decentering that is most important. It is important because it complicates our notions of meaning; we can assume nothing.

This interpretation can apply on multiple levels in education. On a macro level, it forces us to recognize that a single educational policy does not work similarly for all schools or students. Hence we can not and should not expect for the same "reform" effort to produce the same results in all schools. On a micro level, a post-structuralist interpretation forces us to examine the center—which ways of knowing do we privilege? Once we answer this question, then we must determine how to de-center certain types of knowledge or certain content areas. For example, how would learning be structured if we did not have "core" subjects (e.g. . .math and science) or what would learning be if we had different "core" subjects (e.g. . .art and music). On a personal level, a post-structuralist interpretation would push us to honor the whole child in serious and consistent ways. In doing so, we would see children consulted (and valued for their opinions) in all facets of their education. We would have children and youth involved in creating and implementing curriculum and policy. Some may ask, "Why ask a five year old what she wants to learn?" I would respond with "Because she is the one who has to learn it." To involve children in such ways is not ludicrous. It is, instead, rooted in a Freirian model of teaching and learning in which the learner is valued for the knowledge s/he brings to the learning environment.

Such an embracing of children in the decision making process does not mean I am advocating for a complete relinquishing of adult control in education. As hooks[4] (2003) and Noblit (1993) both suggest, being overly permissive does not create the most constructive learning environment. Adults have to accept responsibility for their role in the educative process. But what Noblit argues is closer to the point I am trying to make here. Adults must exercise power in the classroom. Children should be respected yet treated as children and not miniature adults. What I am suggesting is that educators actually consult children when making decisions which will affect their learning and that children's voices have the potential to change reality[5] In my experience, children and youth are rarely consulted in the decision making process and when they are, their opinions have little or no effect on the outcome. To have voice ultimately means that what one says might actually change one's circumstances.

To counter this belief that children should be able to effectively alter their reality, I have heard some educators, administrators, and politicians say that children are only interested in changing the superficial reality. Students, for example, would only have interest in changing the lunch schedule (which I would argue is not so superficial) and would not express interest in curricular matters. Or, the more common argument I hear is that children are not interested in learning the material that will be tested on the end of year standardized test. Real teaching, these critics argue, is about getting children motivated to learn what they have no desire to learn. I like to counter this point with a thought. . . "How amazing would learning be if children could actually learn something they want to learn?" And why do we believe that the two (what we want and what children want) mutually exclusive? If indeed they are, I suggest we take an introspective look at the way we construct curriculum and the way we do education rather than assuming that the fault lies with the children (and their parents).

POST-FORMALISM

Post-formalism can serve as a bridge between postmodern and post-structural discourse. Post-formal thinking, with its demand that we perceive of identity as multiple and power as contextualized creates the discursive space for the ambiguous and the contradictory. It, therefore, allows us to understand democratic public education in tandem with identity — both are active verbs, reflective of process and praxis. I thus begin to end this chapter with several questions and hope that, somehow, in answering these questions we may begin to transform our educational practices in significant ways. Since Lacan's concept of jouissance has been interpreted as "whatever gets you off," I thought it appropriate to apply that question to educational theory. This question is intriguing to me because I remember, as an undergraduate student in education, questioning my professors' persistent articulation of educational theory. I was much more interested in the "practical" aspect of teaching. At the time, I sincerely believed that practice and theory were separate and that I could become a fabulous teacher without all of that nonsensical theory. Of course, now, thirteen years later, I rely on theory to inform my practice. I do so because theory facilitates my understanding of the structure of education—the ways in which public schools, teaching, and learning are organized. Theory grounds my knowledge of the varied and competing paradigms which frame public education. Such paradigms inevitably affect the people who create, maintain, and resist current practices in schools.

But I remain skeptical of theory. Have we reached a point of jouissance in public education? Are we so immersed in theoretical discourses that we are only concerned with those that seem "right" to us, those that "get us off"? I consider myself liberal in my political orientation. But does that mean that "conservative" ways of viewing education have nothing to offer? I am no longer sure I can define liberal or conservative in meaningful ways. I am confident, however, that theory should also be grounded in practice and that we ought to be able to teach in ways that create/nurture/shape critical capacities in our students. And, perhaps most importantly, I have never met a teacher who believes that standardized tests should be the primary measure of student ability.

So, how might Lacanian theory apply to public education in the U.S. and how might it do so in ways that make schools places where students want to be? First, I believe that we should set aside considerable time for developing and nurturing the psychological and emotional well being of students. We can no longer assume that the home is the only place such support should occur nor should we assume that teachers can just accomplish such nurturing "on the side" or whenever they get around to it. If we presume that schools should be a place where we care for the "whole child," then we have to ask ourselves how we do so and in what specific ways do we do so? And how is such care assessed or evaluated? If we are to espouse what Noddings (2001) terms an "ethic of care," then how do we know that such care is an integral part of the school day and not merely implemented as simplistic character education traits of the month? Can we ask to see teachers' lesson plans and see care specifically addressed as a learning objective? This might sound crazy and, even as I write it, seems to sound just a bit too positivist. But, my point is only that, if we claim it is important for students to learn/know, we need to have some evidence that teachers and administrators are thinking critically about how to teach it and how to assess students' learning of it. Because Lacan believed that each patient's subjectivity emerged in the space of psychoanalytic sessions which specifically sought to decode the unconscious, I similarly suggest that, if we want students to become more compassionate and caring human beings, schools must incorporate such ideas into the curriculum, develop specific teaching and learning objectives, and create meaningful ways to assess student learning.

Equally important, we could use Lacanian theory as a way to facilitate our embracing of ambiguity and mystery. For Lacan, the unconscious served as the locus of the subject. If we think of teaching and learning as the relationship between/within language and as a relationship that thrives in the unknown, then we can alter the educative environment by changing the way we assess and evaluate students as well as student learning. Rather than selecting one hundred random questions to ask students about the whole of U.S. history, we might allow them to self construct a narrative which describes the creation of and development of the United States of America. Yes, it would be difficult to "grade." But, I believe that it would allow for students to construct more intriguing narratives about the development of the U.S. and, in doing so, would allow students more opportunity to critically examine the nation in which they live. And, it would allow them the freedom to select and discuss those people and events that they believe to be most interesting in the course of U.S. development. Such a selection process and its subsequent narrative would work well with either a postmodern, post-stucturalist, or post-formal interpretation of education—all of which embrace ambiguity and search for stories that are outside of dominant paradigms—because the narrative process would give students the opportunity to speak about people who are not considered part of the "canon" of U.S. history.

And finally, Lacan's belief that subjects are constructed in language allows us, as educators, to ground our understanding of children in the way they speak and write about themselves. If we work from a Lacanian perspective, then we would find specific ways to listen to children (as well as our colleagues). And, we would attune ourselves to the intricacies of speech. In doing so, we could construct classrooms or learning environments in which students know that we are listening and, as a result, thoughtfully consider their words before, during, and after speaking. In such an environment, students would have the space and time to evaluate the teacher as listener while the teacher evaluated the students in similar fashion. Students and teachers could thus enter into dialogue with each other and, hopefully, preclude many possible "negative" behaviors or circumstances which might impede learning.

Ultimately, Lacan's theories (those that I have briefly discussed here) remind us of the mystery in education. He illuminates for us the multiple possibilities inherent in the unknown and the joy in searching for those possibilities. In addition, analyzing Lacan with postmodern, post-structural, and post-formal paradigms reminds us that we must begin teaching wary of prescribed solutions because to embrace such prescriptions is to ignore the complexities of personality, power, and place. Using Lacan does not mean that we uncritically embrace his theories, many of which are convoluted and themselves ambiguous, but it does mean that we remain cognizant of the attention we must pay to the personal and political.

NOTES

[1] Drive, in this sense, refers to the death drive. Freud's commentary on this concept came in 1933 when he and Albert Einstein exchanged letters addressing the question, "Why war?" In his responses, Freud suggested that man was instinctively aggressive and bound to a quest for death.

---

[2] Cited in Fink, 2004, p. 124 and in Lacan's seminar "The purloined letter"

[3] Of course I understand that we teach our students the value of silence when it is necessary to listen. Here, when I use the term silencing, I am referring to the constructing of authoritarian classrooms that do not embrace student voice, classrooms constructed by teachers who do not believe that students should be a part of the decision making process.

[4] bell hooks, cultural critic, does not capitalize her name.

[5] I base this idea on bell hooks' (2005) belief that the ability to manipulate one's gaze to change reality was and is part of an exercise of power for black women.

CHAPTER 6

LACAN ENACTED: TRUTH AND RECONCILIATION, CURRICULUM, & PEDAGOGY

Applying Lacan's theories to curriculum is challenging, to say the least. But, his theories do provide some indelible possibilities for public education in the twenty-first century. Considering his relevance to post-structuralism, post-formalism, post colonialism, and postmodernism, a Lacanian perspective of public education would defy the current standardization of curriculum in the wake of No Child Left Behind mandates. Using Lacan, I envision public education as a process which encourages the distinctiveness of students, challenges normative assumptions about what a "good" student is, and demands that teachers facilitate student understanding of multiple truths but that teachers also engage in an honest reconstruction of history—one that acknowledges the brutality of conquest, the arrogance of imperialism, and the illusiveness/elusiveness of peace. Although I dare not provide a Lacanian model of public education (to do so would be, I believe, as I have said in earlier chapters, contrary to the spirit of Lacan), I will offer, in this chapter, a few possibilities for public education enacted in a post-formal Lacanian framework.

To begin, I suggest that we consider/reconsider what the primary purpose(s) of public education are or should be. Public education has to have some relevance to the common good; otherwise, why call it public education? And, these purposes or common good must be defined (albeit broadly). Although post-formal and postmodern thinking challenges specific definitions because they have a tendency towards reification, some specificity is necessary for political purposes; it helps us collaborate with cohesiveness and to work more effectively towards education that somehow brings more meaning to people's lived experiences. To this end, I will use Parker Palmer's explanation of the purposes of education to provide a framework for understanding what our larger common goals as educators/potential educators should be. He says, "Education is about healing and wholeness. It is about empowerment, liberation, transcendence, about renewing the vitality of life. It is about finding and claiming ourselves and our place in the world" (as cited in hooks, 2003, p. 43). In this respect, education connects our personal lives to the political and social context in which we live.

Palmer's conception of education, understood from a Lacanian perspective, would mirror the role/function of psychoanalysis — to translate the unconscious in an effort to uncover the "self" understanding that this "self" is completely bound in language and relationship (to people and the environment). Perhaps more specifically, Palmer's belief that education is about "finding and claiming our place in the world" complements Lacan's expectation that psychoanalysis would help us distinguish between the projected "I" that we believe to be the conscious self and the hidden, yet speaking, "I" of the unconscious subject. Our "place in the world" has as much to do with our place in relationship to others and the world as it does to our relationship to our "selves." And, in a philosophical way, the unlocking of the unconscious represents a search for truth, the truth of the subject or self.

Because Palmer's definition of education and Lacan's psychoanalytic process center on this philosophical quest for truth and because each makes specific connections between one's personal journeys and the larger socio-political context, I center my Lacanian vision of public education on the concept "truth and reconciliation" and will make further connections between the process of truth and reconciliation and curriculum and pedagogy. Although there have been some spirited debates about the nature of truth (including the classical Greek Philosophers, Socrates, Plato, and Aristotle, German philosophers Georg Wilhelm Friedrich Hegel and Friedrich Nietzsche, Danish philosopher Søren Kierkegaard, as well as Asian and African philosophical traditions of Kong Fuzi (Confucius) and Shaihu Usman dan Fodio (Nigerian, Islamic philosopher—the list could go on indefinitely), I fundamentally believe that "truth" exists, that it serves as the impetus for social justice, and that it, in its simplest form forces us to sacrifice personal gain for the common good. For my purposes, truth is socially constructed (see constructivist theory) and rooted in history, social relationships, and processes. And while there may not be one version of truth upon which everyone agrees, there are versions of truth which promote the betterment of humankind—i.e. the end of oppression, violence, poverty, and apathy.

TRUTH AND RECONCILIATION

In 1995, the Truth and Reconciliation Commission was established in South Africa as a way to begin the post-apartheid healing process. Considering the deeply rooted and long history of racism and oppression is South Africa, the Commission began its work in what seemed like an impossible position. One of the commission's primary purposes was to bear witness to and record the statements of victims. The commission also heard the testimony of perpetrators of violence and decided whether or not to grant those individuals amnesty. At its inception, therefore, the TRC served as an official body which would create spaces for people (victims and perpetrators) to speak their truths. In retrospect, many people question the success of the TRC, particularly victims who felt that the commission should not have granted perpetrators amnesty. Because, however, the process required the creation of spaces for truth telling and forced the coming together of seemingly polar opposite groups, it grounds my re-envisioning of public education in the United States.

If we are to create a public education system dedicated to educational processes which support healing and wholeness, then we must construct educational structures (both ideological and physical) which support and nurture the speaking and hearing of truth. This means that textbooks and teachers must avoid neutrality and, instead of teaching "just the facts," teach the social and historicized context of "facts." In practice, then, when teaching math, we would begin with the multiple and varied concepts of math, using, for example, the Mende method for addition or the ancient Egyptian method of multiplication. When teaching science, we would never teach science divorced from its ethical or moral implications. An energy lesson, for example, would naturally include instruction on conservation. Similarly, an economics lesson on capitalism would speak to the problems associated with capitalism instead of only speaking to the benefits of competition. Because the math lesson would promote more complicated conceptual thinking about math and present students with mathematical concepts from non-western countries, and because the energy and economics lessons would connect moral and ethical dilemmas to the presentation of "factual data," each of these lessons would force us to introduce students to critical thinking in socially responsible ways. Such lessons support education for healing and wholeness and uncover truths which lead to the end of oppression, violence, poverty, and apathy.

Constructing curricula which provide socio-historicized constructions of truth requires an acceptance of ambiguity and an ability to teach that ambiguity without teaching moral relativism (the belief that "everything is ok."). "Everything is not "ok"—every perspective is not "ok." In the curriculum I am suggesting, it is not ok, for example, to accept capitalism on an "as is" basis. The widening gap between rich and poor, the inability of many families to economically survive (much less, compete), and the millions of children living in poverty are all unacceptable results of capitalism. In creating a curriculum dedicated to truth and reconciliation, we must, therefore, begin with some moral position. And though many will cringe at the word and will argue that making such definitive claims is antithetical to the principles of post-modernism and post formalism, I do not interpret either theory to mean that we embrace/accept any "truth." Both theoretical frameworks embrace multiple truths and demand that we learn to hear and understand the alternate discourses of oppressed people. They do not suggest, however, that we accept discourses which maintain the dominant power structure or systems/processes/structures that oppress.

If I were to create a moral position statement which could be used as a framework for curricula development in public schools, it would begin with Parker Palmer's definition of the purpose of education (to promote healing and wholeness) and would include (at the minimum) the following corollary expectations:

1. Education promotes critical thinking and supports the development of problem-solving skills in students. Process is emphasized above product.

2. Content is important only if it is relevant to students lived experiences and/or understanding of themselves as individuals connected to a larger social context.

3. Instruction is integrated, never compartmentalized into isolated subjects (e.g. science, history, or art).

4. Assessment is used a way of encouraging student self reflection and to determine better methods of integrating instruction.

5. Students psychological well-being and social growth are studied and evaluated (with their input) on a regular basis.

6. Students are taught to live in community (in local, national, and global contexts) and with respect to the environment.

7. Power is shared and decisions are made (on all levels), democratically and with consensus.

If these were fundamental expectations of public education, then we could not define student achievement in only quantitative ways nor could we fall victim to standardized testing as the primary means of assessing student learning. And while I do not suggest that the seven expectations listed above are new or groundbreaking (educational theorists since John Dewey have suggested such for decades), I am claiming that any effort to "reform" public schools curricula begin and end with these goals.

EDUCATION AS WORK: CHALLENGING THE NOTION OF PLAY

So, if we are to consider the seven principles listed above as the framework for public education, then we must also re-envision what students actually do in public schools. Obviously, it is not enough to have a few idealistic principles posted bravely on the walls of our "ideal" school. We must, in addition, imagine what education would look like in our democratically framed school. To do so, I will use the work of Maria Montessori, Italian psychiatrist and educational theorist. Her work has spawned the creation of numerous schools claiming to implement the Montessori method. Cossentino (2006) elaborates on the Montessori method and notes that it challenges the work of play theorists (e.g...Beatty, 1995 and Kramer, 1976) by using the term "work" to refer to children's activity instead of "play." This shift in descriptive language creates a different understanding of and engagement with children, teaching, and learning. More specifically, Cossentino says,

> Montessori placed deliberate and emphatic emphasis on the concept of work. From the holistic project of development to the very ideal of active, purposeful engagement, work is cast as the means as well as the end of Montessori education . . . In considering the rhetorical possibilities of work as an educational construct, I conclude that Montessori did, indeed, introduce a new conception of work to the lexicon of education. It is a holistic or 'cosmological' (Cossentino 2004 & 2005) conception that reaches for individual as well as universal 'goodness,' casting reform as an intellectual, and moral/act (p. 64).

Cossentino goes on to discuss the ways in which Maria Montessori was criticized when her notion of work was first introduced and contrasted with the play theory of German educational theorist Froebel (who provided a concept of the kindergarten). While critics attacked her method for ignoring the natural tendencies of the child, she argued that it embraced those tendencies. Cossentino sums up Montessori's conception of work and its applicability to the child by saying,

> Work, in a Montessori environment is child, rather than teacher, directed. It is designed to 'set free' rather than mold the child's personality. Because it is driven by a natural desire to develop through exploration and eventually mastery, work, in this scheme, is also joyful, even a 'site of optimal experience,' (Csikszentmihaly, 1990; Rathunde, 2001). Yet the differences between play and work are just as pronounced. The defining conditions of work are that it is both natural and effortful. Work is not an escape from 'real life,' but rather a path towards its fulfillment (p. 68).

There are obvious differences in connotation between the words "work" and "play." For our purposes here, however, I focus on the specific purposefulness that the word "work" evokes. While I do not believe that play is purposeless, I do believe that work denotes (whether consciously or subconsciously), particular purpose. There is a reason for doing "work." There is not necessarily a reason for "play." Because I envision public education devoted to creating integrated human beings with meaning and collective purpose in life (for the social good), I favor the use of the term "work" when describing education.

My evocation of the term is taken, I hope, in the spirit of Montessori's work – that teaching and learning is conducted with a cognizance of purpose. And, to take this concept further, I refer to the work of Noblit (1993) who, when describing the pedagogy of one particular African American teacher, comments that this particular teacher remains fully aware of her presence and authority in the classroom and, while she may create democratic spaces for her children to engage and participate in the learning process, she takes seriously her role as the teacher/guide/facilitator in the classroom. She does not forsake this authority to create a pedagogy of permissiveness. Such pedagogy would lead to unconstructive chaos and would, in essence, inhibit teaching and learning. Nor does she, in contrast, wield her authority like a nicely sharpened blade, ready to slash the student who would challenge it. Instead, she exercises power with care, always attune to the needs of her students.

Equally important, Montessori believed that work would allow for some normalcy in the child's development. From a postmodern or post formal perspective, this drive towards "normalcy" reeks of standardization and seems antithetical to the counter-hegemonic distinctiveness we hope students develop. But, there are some important points that I am willing to concede –1) For communities/societies to function in some sort of coherent way, most members must be willing to subscribe to some cultural "norms," 2) Belief in these cultural norms supports collective action or inaction, and 3) To create a society committed to equity and justice, there must be a collective embracing of some "ideals" as part of its cultural expectations or norms. In other words, we all collaborate in some way; to consciously do so requires a careful balancing of our personal and collective identities.

Montessori's training and interest in adolescent psychology, when used to explain her emphasis on the "normalcy" of child development, offers a complicating twist for our understanding of democratic education in a postmodern and post-formal framework. In juxtaposing her emphasis on normalcy with postmodern and post-formal emphasis on difference, we face the tension between such normalcy (that which we need to participate in a community and to be accepted as a member that understands that community's cultural expectations) and difference (the individuality we claim as a vital part of our uniqueness). Similarly, we face this tension when assessing the importance/impact of NCLB legislation. Standardization of the curriculum and the processes which support such standardization are now the norm and any critique of such processes is generally considered, presumed to be based in democratic thought. But, without any accountability, historically oppressed groups could remain forever oppressed – NCLB (for all of its faults), for example, has brought into public debate the vast differences in educational opportunities for students of color and white students, poor students and affluent students (although, students of color and poor students have known for quite some time that they were not receiving an "equal" education).

If we consider Montessori's conception of work in a Lacanian framework, then we could argue that the "work" of education is similar to the "work" of psychoanalysis; each requires purposeful activity and each presumes that there is a normalcy to being (otherwise, there would be no label such as "abnormal behavior"). So, while I am hesitant to claim the term "normalcy," I also believe/hope that equity and justice will become fundamental to curricula in public schools. For this to happen, they must enter the collective imagination as a part of our cultural norm; they must become part of what we believe to be "common sense" or accepted, normative traditions (Gramsci, 1971). Such a transformation requires an ideological shift or, in Gramscian terms, a war of position (cultural/ideological war). As such, it requires an in depth analysis of our media, political structures, and social institutions (e.g...public schools) because such processes/structures work collaboratively to create a collective consciousness which, in turn, shapes what we believe is "common sense." So, how do we transform such a consciousness? I believe such a transformation begins with our public educational system(s).

GEOGRAPHIC EDUCATION AND ITS RELEVANCE TO CURRICULUM TRANSFORMATION

When I began my career as a high school social studies teacher twelve years ago, I had just emerged from an undergraduate collegiate experience which stressed the interconnectedness of the world. As an assistant professor at a state university located in North Carolina, I face/embrace an institutional charge to create powerful learning experiences for our students while also preparing them to be global citizens. Though I am excited to work at an institution that has a sense of international responsibility, I am also troubled by the fact that it seems we (as a nation) have moved so slowly in bringing such a goal to our students in K-12 public schools. Our continued struggles over bilingual education (including a dismissal of it, by many, as important or necessary), our inability to make teaching of foreign languages mandatory and consistent throughout K-12, and our inability to make study abroad a fundamental part of the curriculum (it is not even required by most state colleges or universities) all reflect a continued rhetoric of global connectedness but we conduct little substantive work to create such understandings as fundamental to our schooling processes. And though we (in North Carolina) have students study world history in high school, there is no corresponding required course on global studies. So it comes as no surprise when I meet students who can not even label the continents on a world map much less the countries, major cities and bodies of water. They know even less about the people and their cultural experiences.

Thus, I turn to Morgan's (2006) discussion of developing geographic wisdom as critical and practical example of how we might implement curricula that charge students with being global intellectual citizens – together, these three terms connect the cultural, critical, and collective responsibilities we need to hold in order to frame a public educational system whose purpose is to create socially responsive students able to critically consider and adapt in ever changing environments. Indeed, the most basic goals of geographic education are education for sustainable development (ESD) and global citizenship (GC). Morgan interprets these as "demanding the dual development of environmental and social/intercultural concern which are both, in turn, predicated upon non-reductive conceptions of justice, moral relevance, and compassionate identification" (p. 336).

Drawing on the work of Griffin (1988), Wilber (1997), O'Sullivan (1999), O'Sullivan & Taylor (2004) and O'Sullivan, et. al. (2002), Morgan also refers to "reconstructive postmodernism" which seeks an "integral vision" from dynamic and evolving perspectives and which ultimately inspires an "integral transformative learning" paradigm. Morgan captures the imminent possibilities of geographic education in the following statement,

> What is being advocated here is the development of a relational mode of 'being in the world' in which multidimensional thinking (Lipman, 2003) is stimulated by and applied to, a world (incorporating both human and 'more than human' dimensions) that is expansively (deeply and richly) perceived, valued and identified with and, ultimately, served. The requirement is for the development of the kind of thinking in which conceptions of justice, moral relevance, and compassionate identification are extended from the merely parochial in the sense of the personal (egocentric); social (ethnocentric); *and* species (anthropocentric) to transpersonal domain of 'more than human' world (Abrams, 1997) (p. 338).

Using Morgan's conceptualization, I envision two particularly fundamental changes to K-12 public education in the U.S. – 1) The study of geography (physical, social, and cultural) would be required, and 2) Geography would be linked to the study of sustainable economic development. Students would learn, from kindergarten through grade 12, geography integrated with the study of culture, ecology, economics, and civics. In this way, geography would serve as a method of connecting social, economic, political theories and religious ideology with students' lived experiences.

Morgan goes on to discuss the re-emergence of wisdom in scholarly discussions among developmental psychologists and it is here that I wish to add yet another layer to the post-formal Lacanian curriculum framework I envision. To review, thus far, I have suggested that we begin with Parker Palmer's definition of the purpose of education (to promote healing and wholeness) and that, when we write curricula, we use the following minimum expectations as the basis:

1. Education promotes critical thinking and supports the development of problem-solving skills in students. Process is emphasized above product.

2. Content is important only if it is relevant to students lived experiences and/or understanding of themselves as individuals connected to a larger social context.

3. Instruction is integrated, never compartmentalized into isolated subjects (e.g. science, history, or art).

4. Assessment is used a way of encouraging student self reflection and to determine better methods of integrating instruction.

5. Students psychological well-being and social growth are studied and evaluated (with their input) on a regular basis.

6. Students are taught to live in community (in local, national, and global contexts) and with respect to the environment.

7. Power is shared and decisions are made (on all levels), democratically and with consensus.

In addition, I have argued that we use the Truth and Reconciliation Commission's (of South Africa, post-Apartheid) processes of creating spaces for the speaking of truth(s) as a model for public school administration and classroom processes. I have suggested also that we use Maria Montessori's concept of work as a way to frame public education because it evokes a certain purposefulness and, as such, allows for the construction of curricula specifically dedicated to the larger social good.

If we add Morgan's construction of wisdom to our curriculum framework, then we push one of the presumed purposes of education – the pursuit of knowledge – to another dimension. Wisdom suggests something beyond knowledge. It calls forth a sense of profound awareness that comes with experience. Morgan (2006, p. 339) refers to Staudinger and Werner's (2003) list of 6 characteristics of wisdom. I will cite them in their entirety here because they provide a critical distinction between what we commonly refer to as knowledge (e.g. "facts") and wisdom:

1. Wisdom deals with important and/or difficult matters of life and the human condition;

2. Wisdom is truly superior knowledge, judgment, and advice;

3. Wisdom is knowledge with extraordinary scope, depth, and balance applicable to specific situations;

4. Wisdom is used for one's good and the good of others;

5. Wisdom combines mind and character; and

6. Wisdom is very difficult to achieve but more easily recognized.

If we use this list as a preliminary way to understand wisdom, then we can reach several conclusions. First, wisdom incorporates knowledge but knowledge does not necessarily lead to wisdom. Second, wisdom reveals the interstices of time and relationship, logic and emotion, individuality and collectivity. With wisdom, one understands these connections; they are naturally and progressively evolving.

Similarly, post-formal thinking presumes that we are constantly learning, that learning is grounded in experience, and that diverse experiences shape one's knowledge construction processes. Wisdom, because it is rooted in its applicability to specific situations, changes depending on one's context. In this sense, then, post-formal thinking is not divorced from reality. It is, rather, grounded in the multiplicity and divergence of various realities. It calls for more than a simple recognition of difference but, instead, an embracing of this distinctiveness as necessary for human evolution in tandem with ecological evolution. In other words, the distinctiveness of humankind matters only in so much as it allows for the evolution of the natural world. It is not enough to be different or to accept difference. We must use our differences to imagine better possibilities for humanity in relationship.

Thus wisdom, because it presumes superior knowledge and allows for judgment and advice, takes us away from the moral relativism I mentioned earlier. All "knowledge" is not acceptable just as all "truths" are not allowable. Some are better equipped to move humankind towards a more just and compassionate relationship with the earth and each other. Wisdom, therefore, is important to the curricular framework I envision because it demands skepticism, judgment, compassion, and knowledge – balanced accordingly, these four processes allow us to claim (or reclaim) a moral position with respect to education. In a post-formal context, wisdom promotes creativity and, consequently, pushes us to consider better ways of being in the world. Ultimately, post-formal thinking demands that we create through dialogue and reflection, that we refute all conceptions/arguments that present the world as either/or and that we dream differently.

What, then, would wisdom be for Lacan? Quite honestly, I am not sure. But, I do know that Lacan, in his analysis of discourse and presumption that Man is a speaking subject through language, does not critique the power structures which shape discourse. So while I believe that wisdom allows us to identify oppression and the power structures that create/maintain it, I do not believe that this was a primary concern for Lacan (other than the power structure he insinuates in the relationship between analyst and analysand). Campbell (2004) further argues,

> One effect of the collapse of these key concepts is that Lacan's concept of the social does not address the complexities of social relations but instead presents them as homogenous. For this reason, Peter Dew rightly argues that the concept of the Symbolic order ignores the relations of domination and oppression within the social world (1987, p. 105-106). For example, the Lacanian account does not address the operations of power upon and within discourse. The theory of the four discourses understands discursive relations between subjects as horizontal, such that each subject is equally powerful. Yet clearly some subject positions are more socially powerful than others, and certain persons more easily able to take up those positions of power (p. 113).

This does not mean that Lacan says nothing of power. Indeed, he recognizes its importance in a philosophical, historical, and analytical sense. He clearly speaks of the exercise of power on the part of the analyst – "Assuredly, a psychoanalyst directs the treatment" (*Écrits*, 586). But, he goes on to argue that psychoanalysts dare not direct the patient. Directing the treatment and directing the patient, therefore, are entirely different. He even acknowledges the effects of cultural beliefs (which are inherently shaped by relationships of power) on the analytic process. Specifically, he says,

> These directives are initially laid out to the patient in the form of instructions which, however little the analyst comments on them, convey, even in the very inflections of this statement of them, the doctrine the analyst himself has arrived at. Which does not mean that the analyst remains unscathed by the mass of prejudices that await him n the patient, based on the idea the latter has been allowed to form of the procedures and aim of the psychoanalytic enterprise by the spreading of notions about analysis in his culture (*Écrits*, 586)

Lacan is simultaneously presumptuous about the ability of psychoanalysts (that they are/can be equipped to draw out the unconscious) and critical of those who claim to be psychoanalysts but who ignore the potential consequences of their assumptions and presence in the process. He was, obviously familiar with the critiques of Marx and Foucault, both of whom clearly speak to the larger social structures which oppress. Indeed, Lacan formed an intellectual relationship with noted Marxist Louis Althusser. Valente (2003) describes this uneasy relationship in this way, "In his pedagogy, Lacan periodically set his own theoretical discoveries in loose analogy to broadly Marxist principles, mainly for the purpose of familiarizing the younger and more politically minded intellectuals at the Ecole with his highly specialized conceptual vocabulary" (p. 159). Althusser, on the other hand, compared Lacan's Imaginary register to that of Marx's concept of ideology. Both the mirror stage in Lacan and ideology in Marx depend upon and create a particular reflexivity which leads to false consciousness.

If we read Althusser's Marxism alongside Lacan's notion of the Symbolic, then we can extrapolate from Lacan some implications for power relations and oppression. Valente goes on to argue that Althusser translated Lacan's Symbolic into the "Law of culture" and, consequently, for our purposes here, brought forth some critical understanding of Lacan's relevance to theories of power. He says,

> Whereas the Imaginary provides Althusser with a unified field theory of alienation, in which individual misrecognition and collective ideological mystification feed (into) one another, the Symbolic provides Althusser with a unified field theory of the still more radical estrangement involved in becoming human in the first place, whether *qua* sexed or fully social being (p. 165).

In other words, individuals, according to Althusser's Marxist interpretation of Lacan, assume a social identity that is externally imposed – they assume the identity that is defined for them by ideology or the culture of the society into which they are born. Lacan, however, was never really a Marxist, so Althusser's interpretations of Lacan are best understood as juxtapositions of theories. Nonetheless, Campbell's (2004) critique remains. Lacan's theory of discourse does not adequately account for or explain the structures/institutions of power that shape discourse.

So, what does this omission mean for us? It simply reminds us that we are using Lacan along with several other theories (e.g...postmodern and post-formal) to imagine a different kind of public school curriculum. It also reminds us of the alienation which occurs during identity formation (remember Lacan's mirror state) and the relationship between that alienation and social structures (whether that be discourse or power). Thus, on a basic level, we must conceive of a way to build an educational system that supports the construction of identity in the Symbolic realm (that of discourse), which recognizes that language is derived in relationships/ systems of power, and which rejects ideological constructions of identity in favor of those which emanate from within the unconscious. Now that sounds like an impossible undertaking.

CONSTRUCTING A CURRICULUM OF AUTHENTIC CONSCIOUSNESS

Obviously, the phrase "authentic consciousness" is a contested one. How do we even begin to define "authentic consciousness" using a post-formal Lacanian lens? Undoubtedly, it is a consciousness that can be multiply defined and is contingent upon one's social and political context(s). It is a consciousness that continually identifies and evaluates ideological paradigms and then uses that knowledge to self assess. It is a consciousness based on the experiential, the circumstantial, and the theoretical. It is evolving, always in process. To construct a curriculum of authentic consciousness thus requires that we learn to live in the process; we understand that learning is as much about knowing ourselves as it is about knowing the "content." So, what does this imply for students and teachers in public school classrooms?

First, it requires that classrooms be about investigation, inquiry, exploration, discovery, and questioning. To do so requires dialogue, reflection, and action – all components of Freire's (1970) notion of praxis. If we were to continue dividing school curricula into content strands (and I am not a proponent of this), then we would construct only that curricula and content which lends itself to such learning and teaching processes. Or (and this is the method I prefer), we could structure curriculum and content around such processes. For example, "investigation" would be the learning strand and we would incorporate various subjects/topics into that strand. Since there are thousands of schools across the nation with mission statements which incorporate the idea of encouraging students to "be lifelong learners," it stands to reason that we are claiming to value the learning process over and beyond the actual content. If this claim is accurate, then it would make sense to restructure curriculum around those processes we believe important – to arrange a curriculum that centers on teaching students how to critically think and construct activities along with that curriculum which creates the space and opportunity for students to do so. In this curriculum, "content" is secondary and learning processes are privileged.

But if we are to facilitate the process of developing an authentic consciousness among our students, we must also center all classes on the idea of praxis—reflective thought and action—and dialogue. Children, of all ages, would have to practice engaging in dialogue with other students. More specifically, they would have to engage in dialogue with students from different communicative backgrounds (hearing students with deaf or hearing impaired students, students for whom English is a second language with students for whom English is the primary language, students from different socio-economic or racial backgrounds, etc.). Of course, it is difficult to create authentic spaces for dialogue when assignments are mandatory. In an effort to create such authentic spaces, we have serious attempts (within the academy) to provide students with service learning experiences.

Service learning, however, has been critiqued since its inception because opponents argue that it creates too many opportunities for privileged students to "Other" those who are not privileged and that, if students are unable to get beyond it being a required part of the course, it does not offer much opportunity for meaningful interaction (e.g. students simply go volunteer because they have to). And while service learning differs from the communicative experiences I have outlined above, the critiques are similar; they are, fundamentally, about how to create meaningful experiences in "Othered" circumstances (e.g. how do you teach students to empathize with poverty? Simply having them work for a few hours in a homeless shelter does not guarantee empathy). Proponents of service learning believe that it can and does create space for authenticity and, therefore, can promote or facilitate powerful learning experiences. Soslau and Yost (2007), drawing upon an array of literature on service learning, argue that,

> Service learning, when designed and implemented appropriately, serves as a way to weave challenging, content-related outcomes through the curriculum in an experiential manner. Authentic instruction in the context of community events leads students to make natural connections between the content they are learning in the classroom and their service-learning experiences (p. 37).

Their emphasis on service-learning as contextualized by the community is an important one. Many of us hope that service learning opportunities will help students connect what they have learned in the classroom to life experiences which may not be their own and we hope that in doing so students make more personal and political connections to the course content. Ultimately, if they do, they may use what they have learned to improve society, to eliminate inequities and injustices.

Of course, not all service learning experiences are equal; some provide greater opportunities for student engagement. Soslau and Yost used the MY VOICE model which emphasizes the incorporation of student voice and democratic processes in the service learning experience. According to Soslau and Yost, this model, created by Need in Deed expects students to be involved in the actual creation of the service learning experience. For our purposes here, I am most concerned with how we can create "authentic" service learning experiences that help students understand the multiple connections between what they have read and real life experiences. So, what does "authentic" mean? The term is used often by educational theorists, used in different ways, and not even always specifically defined. It is rooted, however, in the Theory of Authentic Learning. Hill and Smith (2005), who base their work in that of Barab and Plucker (2002), highlight four major components of authentic instruction: mediation, embodiment, distribution, and situatedness. Mediated learning occurs when students use cultural tools (e.g. language), embodiment recognizes that body learning is just as important as cognitive; distribution implies that learning is a collective process, and situatedness means that learning occurs in context and that what is learned in one context is not necessarily transferable to another.

Similarly, Harland (2005) takes Authentic Learning Theory and uses it to outline the development of a portfolio for teachers in a teacher education program. In this context, he defines authentic inquiry as being comprised of "teachers constructing their own theories of practice," "education that emphasizes the freedom to learn from experience," and "learning as a form of practitioner research" (p. 329). Authentic, thus implies that one has the freedom and opportunity to construct the learning experience. Equally important, Abbott (2005) defines authentic learning as that which occurs at the nexus between the classroom and the world. Occurring in this nexus, authentic learning, at its best, allows for the seamless integration of knowledge from multiple contexts (e.g…the classroom and the "real" world). While I do not believe that classroom experiences are divorced from "real" world experiences (after all, the school and its classrooms are a part of the "real" world"), I am discussing them here as separate entities because that is how they are often discussed in popular culture.

I would like to think that Lacan would agree that learning should be grounded in "real" world experiences. The work of psychoanalysts, in particular, depends on people's lived experiences. Psychoanalysts take the discourse of the subject, which is an interpretation of their experience, and apply what they "know" to the process of analysis. In this relationship, there is no separation of theory from the lived experience. In particular, psychoanalysts use the body and its symptoms as a way to understand or hear the unconscious. So, the idea of embodiment as it corresponds to authentic learning resembles the method of symptom identification/recognition in psychoanalysis. In authentic learning and psychoanalysis, the body is a speaking body, one capable of bringing forth various truths which the "mind" or conscious self rejects. Thus the body becomes a metaphor and vehicle for truth and allows authentic learning to occur (about one's self and one's collectives).

Service learning, as an example (when it is designed and done well) of authentic learning, enables us to construct curriculums which lead to authentic consciousness because it affords us the opportunity to engage with other people's reality and to face truths (of others and ourselves) that we would prefer to avoid. In the facing of these truths, we come to know ourselves and others in more intimate ways and are able to articulate our purpose more specifically. In this way, we come closer to Parker Palmer's definition of education – as being about healing and wholeness. I must add here that this process, of healing and wholeness, applies to teachers and students; unless teachers are engaged in authentic learning, they can never appropriately facilitate the learning of students in authentic ways. This is an important point. Teachers can not teach what they do not know. If we do not work to create authentic learning experiences for ourselves, we will never face our own difficult truths (or the truths of other people's realities) and we will never come to understand what it means to live/be in community.

CARE THEORY, SPIRITUALITY, AND CURRICULUM: CAN WE REALLY TEACH CHILDREN TO CARE?

When Carol Gilligan put forth a systematic delineation of care theory in 1982 and contrasted this theory to male-centered theories of justice, she initiated an international debate about the role/purpose of care in education. How do we design curricula that teach children to care? Is caring innate or can it be taught/learned? If we can teach it, how do we help students "live" other people's circumstances (e.g...service learning) knowing that this "living" is an artificial one (they can disengage from it at any moment)? When Noddings (2001) extends care theory, she attempts to bring it into more current context and make it more specific. She explains, for example, that teachers who espouse an ethic of care engage in behavior that is receptive, related, and engrossed. They center their relationships with students on dialogue which builds trust among students and, indeed, makes them feel free to "be" themselves.

When considering the experiences of students who are members of historically oppressed groups, care theory and its dependence on building trust in relationship, is problematic. If as Tatum (1997) has argued, Black people and other people of color have inherited a legacy of racism, then that inheritance predisposes them/us to operating with a hermeneutic of suspicion. This hermeneutic of suspicion teaches Black people to distrust as a means of physical and psychological survival. When one is externally defined as "Other" and forced into stereotypical associative definitions created by white supremacist thinking (see hooks, 2003), it behooves one to distrust; such distrust becomes a way to maintain distance from those who oppress and to create semi-safe spaces in which to build solidarity among similarly oppressed people. So, how do we resolve this tension in care theory such that the basic premise of care theory – to create schools dedicated to developing caring students who understand how to live as empathetic citizens in communities –still serves useful purposes to educators?

I believe it begins with understanding that we have normative assumptions about care, trust, and respect. These normative assumptions prevent us from understanding that care, trust, and respect are deeply contextualized and historicized. As such, they shape/manipulate people's lived experiences in very different ways. But, above all else, care begins with someone having an interest in another's life. Obviously, some interest is superficial, but, if we implement a curriculum based on an ethic of care, then we are continually and systematically, trying to move students (and ourselves) from a place of superficiality towards authenticity (understanding authenticity as a process, always evolving). In this process, we build trust by coming to know one another and each other's circumstances. We come to learn that trust and care are not absolute concepts; they are, instead, richly layered. For people of color and other groups who know oppression, an ethic of care brings the possibility to "suspend" distrust – to not live with it as a primary lens for viewing the world, but as a secondary one. As a black woman educator, I am always hesitant to completely let go of my distrust, by I do suspend it on occasion. I do so when time, place, and situation come together to create a space in which I feel able to do so without losing my "self." Similarly, I believe an ethic of care and a hermeneutic of suspicion need not be mutually exclusive.

An ethic of care, applied consistently to curricula, should create spaces for students to speak their distrust. Speaking this distrust into public space allows for collective engagement with it; it allows white people, for example, who claim to be "not racist," an opportunity to hear the term "privilege" and to understand how they benefit from it (whether consciously or unconsciously). White students should, with a care curriculum, feel able to speak their belief (e.g...to say "I am not to blame for the racism you experience") and they should come to hear when students of color say, "No, you are not to blame, but you still benefit from racial privilege."). If students and teachers have had time to develop some space of trust (Noddings emphasizes that trust building requires significant time and work), then, each group (in my example, white students and students of color) should be open to hearing the other. With an ethic of care, however, we are still faced with the challenge of rejecting some "truth(s)." This means that language that belittles or degrades another is not tolerated. It means that we teach with the premise of equity (not equality) – every group or person does not get "the same" amount of space or time to speak. We do, instead, acknowledge the history of oppression in the United States (and the world) and allow *more* speaking time for those who belong to oppressed groups.

Immediately, I feel the resistance to this statement. Some will argue that it sounds too much like affirmative action policies and they believe these policies only create "reverse racism." I like to use a practical example here – if school x only spends $2, 000 per pupil and school y spends $10,000, we would all (I hope) understand the inequity in this difference. How can we expect both schools to prepare students similarly without having access to the same material resources? In addition, if the majority of students in school x live below the federal poverty level, and the majority of students in school y come from affluent backgrounds, the resource gap widens. If we were to come along and attempt to "even out the playing field," would it be enough to simply give each school the same amount of money? Not really…such an effort does not necessarily correct the circumstances created by years of inequities nor does it account for the differences in socio-economic backgrounds of families. What difference does it make, for example, if my school has the latest technology if I am homeless and have no place to study? So, while I will not delve into a critique here of liberal democracy and I will not advocate for democratic socialism, I do contend that schools which operate with an ethic of care must create more spaces for students from historically oppressed groups to voice/to speak.

Practically, however, how do we infuse care into our curricula? One such attempt has been in character education. I cringe when I hear of "Character education" programs. My experience with them has been dismal, at best. The administration, perhaps with nominal help from faculty, selects the "character traits." We then celebrate/emphasize them once a month. Children get rewarded for being kind or showing respect. Typically, it descends into children simply engaging in the behavior to get the reward. Rarely, if ever, are the "traits" analyzed with any complexity. Let us take "respect" as an example. Many of the urban children I taught believed that one earned respect. It was not necessarily automatically given to elders or to teachers. If they believed that a teacher did not respect them, they chose willfully not to learn (see Kohl, 1994). Some teachers, in turn, interpreted this "willed not-learning" as a disinterest in learning and, consequently, considered these students unteachable and disposable. In this context, respect must be taught in a more complicated way. The same is true of "honesty." If we consider honesty with a hermeneutic of suspicion, it takes on different meaning. Why would a student be honest if such honesty will result in an attack on her/his character or an invasion in one's home (e.g…the intervention of social service personnel)? Honesty is not absolute and it is not immune from social and political power structures.

Though I distrust character education programs, I do not believe that teaching character or morality or ethical behavior should remain a part of the hidden curriculum or simply taught whenever we get around to it. If children are to learn to be good citizens, we have to define what that means and to assess their learning of it. We cannot assume that abiding by the rules reflects their learning of good citizenship or stewardship. So I do believe that we need to define "good character" and then articulate the complexities of the qualities we have selected. In doing so, we will, hopefully, teach our children to critically think and apply concepts according to different situations.

In addition, I do not believe that we teach character as distinct from spirituality. For me, spirituality denotes a deep relationship between us and the world. For a more specific understanding of spirituality, I turn to Dillard, Abdur-Rashid, and Tyson (2000) who specify the importance of spirituality to educators. Quoting from an interview with Dillard, they say,

> What is spirituality in education? Spirituality in education is education with purpose, education that is liberatory work, education that is emancipation . . . What is spirituality in education? Spirituality in education is education that connects, education that is about building relationships between and across teachers and students, males and females, Others and Ourselves . . . (p. 447).

It comes as no surprise to me that the emergence of a spiritual discourse of education comes, predominantly, from Black women educators who find themselves displaced in the Cartesian model of teaching and learning. Such a model, based on Descartes' comment "I think, therefore I am," separates the mind from the heart, intellect from emotion. The Cartesian model presumes that such a separation is possible and privileges the "mind" over the "heart." Thus we are challenged to make "rational/logical" decisions that are divorced from ethical or moral concerns. If we were to use Ubuntu logic, we would believe, "I am in relationship, therefore I am." Such a shift in thinking would dramatically change the way to think about and do public education in the U.S.

Dillard, Abdur-Rashid, and Tyson suggest that Black women have an inherited cultural framework which centers spirituality and that this framework has been and continues to help them refute institutional structures and processes that oppress and silence their voices. They challenge us to consider this cultural framework, with spirituality as central, and to use it as a way to facilitate the creation of culturally relevant pedagogy. Ladson-Billings (1994) argues that teachers should be culturally competent and, as such, able to provide culturally relevant pedagogy to the students they teach. She defines the culturally competent teacher as one who: "1. Understands culture and its role in education, 2. Takes responsibility for learning about students' culture and community, 3. Uses culture as a basis for learning, and 4. Promotes a flexible use of students' local and global culture (p. 98). She then describes culturally relevant pedagogy as that which 1. Focuses on students' academic achievement, 2. Develops student's cultural competence, and 3. Fosters students' sense of sociopolitical consciousness" (pp. 143-144). Accordingly, cultural competence demands that teachers know and understand the social and political contexts of their students and schools. And, they must go beyond understanding; they must use that understanding to shape their curriculum and pedagogy.

A culturally relevant pedagogy thus allows for the integration of spirituality into the curriculum. While I am not suggesting that teachers indoctrinate students to particular formal religions, I am suggesting that spirituality – education with purpose, education that is libratory work, education that is emancipation – would facilitate the teaching of care and would allow us to construct curricula that have meaning to students' lives. Using Dillard's definition of spirituality, education that is infused with the spiritual would be liberating and, as such, would allow us to transcend oppression. And in this transcendence, we might finally be able to see/think/hear differently. We might be able to create a world without poverty, hopelessness, destructiveness, and war. These are not inevitable (some would argue that they are a part of human nature). They are only inevitable because we do not know how to think beyond them.

A pedagogy constructed within a spiritual framework is what O'Malley (2007) calls pedagogy of the soul. And while it has infinite potential for transcendence, it does not come without particular dangers. A pedagogy of the soul allows us to teach as integrated beings whose presence is imbued with the personal and the political. But because a pedagogy of the soul requires constant grief work (working with the loss of one's self, a psychological consequence of oppression) and demands application to the political, it can have profound and detrimental effects on teachers who come from historically oppressed groups. African American teachers, for example, have historically held a belief that, beyond educating students, their work as educators should uplift the race (Cecelski, 1994). With this belief, they view their teaching as a political enterprise and as such, it could transform the social context. But, for them such a pedagogy demands too much – it requires that they sacrifice for the good of their students and their race. An ethic of care with a pedagogy of the soul leads to what I refer to as "care-sickness"—caring too much, sacrificing irrevocably, and losing one's self for the social good.

When teachers adopt a pedagogy of the soul, it troubles me even though I believe in its powerful capabilities. I am troubled because a pedagogy of the soul can translate, for some, into a pedagogy of sacrifice and adopting the mantra of sacrifice can be quite dangerous in public schools for several reasons, 1. The teacher assumes that s/he should give up everything to save one student (and that student might not even care), 2. The teacher is willing to do anything, accept any administrative nonsense "for the good of the student," and 3. The teacher accepts the bulk of the responsibility when/if the student fails. Such sacrifices strip teachers of their sense of agency and lead then to believe that their needs should always come last. Why is this dangerous? As a practice, it contributes to the de-professionalization of teachers—they/we are expected to sacrifice, to put the students' needs "before" our own, and to embrace any reform effort which claims to be "child-centered." De-profesionalization also leads us to resist collective organizing. Some of us dare not join the union, dare not protest, dare not strike because we have internalized the belief that our needs are less important.

Instead, many of leave the profession. According to the National Education Association (NEA), almost fifty percent of teachers leave the profession within the first five years. And, a report from Barnes, Crowe, and Schaefer (2007) with the National Commission on Teaching and America's Future estimates that this turnover rate costs us several billion dollars per year (their study includes teachers who transfer to other schools within districts as well as those that leave the profession because, they estimate, that such moves still cost districts thousands of dollars per teacher). Although the costs are astronomical, I am not surprised. Low pay and difficult working conditions send new teachers away from the profession in droves and this trend is even worse at schools in urban neighborhoods with high numbers of students of color, low income students, and/or low test scores. In their report, the National Commission on Teaching and America's Future suggests that policy makers add a point on teacher retention to No Child Left Behind legislation.

With states already struggling to meet NCLB mandates and with many states facing budgetary deficits, I doubt that adding such a mandate to the legislation will spark any significant improvement in the near future.

As I write this chapter, I am struck by the irony of this situation. I teach prospective teachers how to build community in the classroom (and the importance of doing so), I teach them about NCLB, it's potential and its shortcomings, and I challenge them to speak in faculty meetings (to not accept the status quo). I know that developing such a voice is difficult, particularly in the face of possible termination if one does not meet one's employer's performance expectations. However, when they leave our program, they are energized, aware of the challenges and ready to face them. So, what happens in that first year? They are inundated with policies, some of which conflict and that do not support their day to day practice in the classroom. They are faced with procedures and processes in the school and district that de-professionalize them and, because they have so much to worry about in the classroom, they have no time to initiate and maintain a professional discourse which refutes such de-professionalization. And there are fewer and fewer veteran teachers left to speak at all.

CRITICAL PEDAGOGY: A POST-FORMAL LACANIAN CURRICULUM?

I have often said that the way we do public education needs radical transformation. McLaren (2003) offers a critique of public education and an explanation of critical pedagogy. Critical pedagogy, in a very broad sense, encompasses the various theories I have briefly described above; it allows us to understand how spirituality and education is important, how caring is necessary, and how culturally relevant pedagogy improves student learning. Critical pedagogy is a theoretical way of thinking and doing education that focuses on teaching students to question and to challenge social and political power structures. It, however, is not just about teaching students to question. In critical pedagogy, we hope to teach students to question processes which maintain racist, sexist, heterosexist, and classist institutions and to analyze how and why such attitudes/behaviors continue to shape the way we do public education, particularly the way we construct curricula. So while critical pedagogy is a way of teaching and learning that embraces student input, creates democratic classroom spaces, and encourages student questioning, it comes wrought with some obvious tensions. Specifically, McLaren says,

> Critical pedagogy directs educators toward a teaching process that . . . often enmeshes us in an ethical and pedagogical dilemma. Critical pedagogy is about power and empowerment. Although this assertion may seem straightforward, in the classroom, it often plays itself out in contradictory ways. On the one hand, the critical educator invites students to construct their own analysis of social phenomena and to appropriate for themselves the process of theory-building. But, on the other hand, the critical educator wants students to situate social phenomena in broader structural relationships and to ask questions, such as who benefits from these relationships, how are unequal

> relationships being reproduced, and how do individuals interpret their situatedness in a system of unequal economic, racial, and gendered relations? For some students, these kinds of questions support their own analysis of social phenomena; for others, they do not. In the latter case, the critical educator often finds himself or herself caught in a dilemma: how to support students' questioning and meaning-making while at the same time teaching students to critique power relations that contextualize schools and place limits on lives (p. xxiii).

So, while I teach my students to question and I embrace such questioning, I face one potential problem – what if my students, in coming to their own conclusions based on their questions, come away with the belief that social inequality does not exist, that all students are capable of achieving anything if they work hard enough, and that teachers' only responsibility is to set high standards and teach the content? And here is the problem. As a secondary social studies methods and foundations of education instructor, I do have an agenda. I am not just here to teach the "content" (however we might define that). I am here to also teach my students how to actively participate in social and political processes because they are connected to multiple communities and affected by the political systems in place; as future educators, I want them to be able to teach students how to engage in/with their communities and more formal political and social systems.

To do so thus requires that we analyze those communities and social and political systems; we have to know what it is we are either enmeshed in or that we might encounter. A Lacanian, post-formal curriculum, at its core, requires that we seek and identify truths, we work to become integrated beings by hearing the unconscious (that which we do not want to or cannot face), and that we understand the limitations on our constructions of self/identity. If we apply these personal requirements to an analysis of the larger socio-political world, them we can translate their applicability to our collective identity building processes. As a collective, or a conglomeration of multiple collectives, what is it that we do not wish to face? How have we constructed a community identity that avoids particular truths? And how has this representation and avoidance marginalized some and made them believe that their truths do not matter?

Ultimately, Lacan's work/theories and post-formalism share several key components—listening, hearing, and interpreting. Applied to public education this means that we should have, in addition to the seven expectations I listed at the beginning of the chapter:

1. Processes in place which allows the space for students and teachers to speak and listen, to build relationships, to discuss the organization of the school, to question the curriculum.

2. Heterarchic rather than hierarchic accountability (dare I say it?). Policy makers, politicians, administrators (all those who structure public education), must create such processes to allow students and teachers to speak and listen and they must be held accountable for doing so. Otherwise, we would have

> nicely worded democratic mission or vision statements and little to no real involvement of teachers and students in the construction of curriculum or organization of schools.

Above all I am a realist. So while I dislike the language of accountability that we currently have driving public education, I also realize that we do need some sort of checks and balances system. Otherwise, how will we ever know that there are actually structures in place in public schools nationwide that allow students and teachers voice and that this voice actually impacts policy making in significant ways? So what will it take to begin to actualize the kind of public schools process I envision? Perhaps we need to revisit the past to better understand the present and future. So, I turn to Franklin Delano Roosevelt's 1933 bank holiday as an example of where we might begin. If we were to use the preliminary suggestions I have outlined in this chapter as a starting point, then we would need to study (listen and hear) from students, teachers, parents, administrators at every school across the nation. To effectively do so, we would need to shut them down for a time period.
Yes, I said it…close the schools. How long would it take to establish democratic processes and curricula particularly suited to the needs of each schools' respective communities? It could take one month, six months, perhaps a year (or longer). While I (particularly as a parent) understand the chaos this would cause — after all, what would parents do with their kids while they worked? — I see absolutely no point in continuing to use our public schools as baby sitting services. If we can suspend public education for a time period and somehow transform it, the time lost during that period would be well worth the superior, more meaningful educational opportunities we could create for our kids. Otherwise, we are, without question, ill preparing them to become critical individuals able to engage in participatory democracy in constructive and consistent ways.

REFERENCES

Abbott, L. (2005). The nature of authentic professional development during curriculum-based telecomputing. *Journal of Research on Technology in Education 37*(4), 379–398.

Allen, P. G., & Anderson, C. D. (2001). *Hozho: Walking in beauty: Native American stories of inspiration, humor, and life*. Chicago: Contemporary Books.

Anyon, J. (2005). *Radical possibilities: Public policy, urban education, and a new social movement.* New York: Routledge.

Apple, M. (1985). *Education and power*. Boston: Ark paperbacks.

Banks, J. (2002). *An introduction to multicultural education*. Boston: Allyn & Bacon.

Berlak, H. (2005). Race and the achievement gap. In H. S. Shapiro and D. E.

Bott, D. (2002). Comment – Carl Rogers and postmodernism: Continuing the conversation. *Journal of Family Therapy, 24*, 326–329.

Braunstein, N. (2003). Desire and jouissance in the teachings of Lacan. In J. M. Rabaté (Ed.), *The Cambridge companion to Lacan* (pp. 102–115). Cambridge: Cambridge University Press.

Campbell, K. (2004). *Jacques Lacan and feminist epistemology*. London: Routledge.

Carlson, D., & Apple, M. (1998). Introduction: Critical educational theory in unsettling times (pp. 1–38). *Power/knowledge/pedagogy: The meaning of democratic education in unsettling times.* Boulder: Westview Press.

Cecelski, D. S. (1994). *Along freedom road: Hyde Country North Carolina, and the fate of black schools in the south.* Chapel Hill: University of North Carolina Press.

Cossentino, J. M. (2006). Big work: Goodness, vocation, and engagement in the Montessori method. *Curriculum Inquiry 36*(1), 63–92.

Dean, T. (2003). Lacan and queer theory. In J. M. Rabaté (Ed.), *The Cambridge companion to Lacan* (pp. 238–252). Cambridge: Cambridge University Press.

Dewey, J. (1902). *The child and the curriculum.* Chicago: University of Chicago Press.

Dewey, J. (1932). *The school and society*. Chicago: University of Chicago Press.

Dillard, C. B., Abdur-Rashid, D., & Tyson, C. A. (2000). My soul is a witness: Affirming pedagogies of the spirit. *Qualitative Studies in Education 13*(5), 447–462.

Edgerton, S. H. (1996). *Translating the curriculum: Multiculturism into cultural studies.* New York: Routledge.

Ellis, D. G. (1991). Post-structuralism and language: Non-sense. *Communication Monographs 58*, 213–224.

Fink, B. (2004). *Lacan to the letter: Reading Écrits closely.* Minneapolis: University of Minnesota Press.

Foucault, M. (1994). *Ethics: Subjectivity and truth.* New York: The New York Press.

Freire, P. (1998a). *Teachers as cultural workers: Letters to those who dare teach.* Boulder: Westview Press.

Gilligan, C. (1982). *In a different voice: Psychological theory and women's development.* Cambridge: Harvard University Press.

Giroux, H. (1988). *Teachers as intellectuals: Toward a critical pedagogy of learning.* Granby, MA: Bergin & Garvey.

Giroux, H. A. (2005). Kids for sale: Corporate culture and the challenge of public schooling. In H. S. Shapiro & D. E. Purpel (Eds.), *Critical social issues in American education: Democracy and meaning in a globalizing world* (3rd ed., pp. 143–162). Mahwah, NJ: Lawrence Erlbaum Associates, Inc.

Gramsci, A. (1971). *Selections from the prison notebooks* (Q. Hoare & G. N. Smith, Eds. & Trans.). New York: International Publishers.

Gutmann, A. (1999). *Democratic education.* Princeton, NJ: Princeton University Press.

Harland, T. (2005). Developing a portfolio to promote authentic teacher enquiry in teacher education. *Teaching in Higher Education 10*(3), 327–337.

Hooks, B. (1994). *Teaching to transgress.* New York: Routledge.

Hooks, B. (2003). *Teaching community: A pedagogy of hope*. New York: Routledge.

REFERENCES

Jagodzinski, J. (2002). The ethics of the "real" in Levinas, Lacan, and Buddhism: Practical implications. *Educational Theory, 52*(1), 81–96.

Kincheloe, J. L., Slaterry, P., & Steinberg, S. R. (2000). *Contextualizing teaching: Introduction to education and educational foundations*. New York: Longman.

Klagas, M. (2001). Jacques Lacan (lecture). Retrieved October 3, 2005 from http://www.colorado.edu/English/ENGL2012Klages/lacan.html

Kohl, J. (1994). "I won't learn from you": And other thoughts on creative maladjustment. New York: New Press.

Kozol, J. (1991). *Savage inequalities: Children in America's schools*. New York: Harper Perennial.

Lacan, J. (1957). Interview. Retrieved October 3, 2005 from http://www.braungardt.com/Psychoanalysis/Lacan-Interview.htm

Lacan, J. (1991a). *The seminar of Jacques Lacan: Book I Freud's papers on technique 1953-1954*. In J.-A. Miller (Ed.) & J. Forrester (Trans.). New York: W. W. Norton & Company, Inc.

Lacan, J. (1991b). *The seminar of Jacques Lacan: Book II The ego in Freud'stheory and the technique of psychoanalysis 1954-1955*. In J.-A. Miller (Ed.) & S. Tomaselli (Trans.) New York: W. W. Norton & Company, Inc.

Lacan, J. (2006). *Écrits* (Bruce Fink Trans.). New York: W. W. Norton & Company.

Lacan, J. (1998). *On feminine sexuality, the limits of love and knowledge, 1972-73/Encore: The seminar of Jacques Lacan Book XX*. (Jacques-Alain Miller, Ed. & Bruce Fink, Trans.). New York: W. W. Norton & Company.

Leicester, M. (2000). Post-postmodernism and continuing education. *International Journal of Lifelong Education, 19*, 73–81.

Lerner, M. (2005). The spiritual transformation of education. In H. S. Shapiro & D. E. Purpel (Eds.), *Critical social issues in American education: Democracy and meaning in a globalizing world* (3rd ed., pp. 325–348). Mahwah, NJ: Lawrence Erlbaum Associates, Inc.

Liu, C. (2003). Lacan's afterlife: Jacques Lacan meets Andy Warhol). In J. M. Rabaté (Ed.), *The Cambridge companion to Lacan* (pp. 253–271). Cambridge: Cambridge University Press.

Lyotard, J. F. (1984). *The postmodern condition: A report on Knowledge (Theory and history of literature, volume X)*. Minneapolis: University of Minnesota Press.

Martin, J. R. (2005). Becoming educated: A journey of alienation or integration? In H. S. Shapiro & D. E. Purpel (Eds.), *Critical social issues in American education: Democracy and meaning in a globalizing world* (3rd ed., pp. 197–210). Mahwah, NJ: Lawrence Erlbaum Associates, Inc.

McLaren, P. (1993). Border disputes: Multicultural narrative, identity formation, and critical pedagogy in postmodern America. In D. McLaughlin & W. Tierney (Eds.), *Naming silenced lives: Personal narratives and the process of educational change*. New York: Routledge.

McLaren, P. (1995). *Critical pedagogy and predatory culture: Oppositional politics in a postmodern culture*. New York: Routledge.

McLaren, P. (2003). *Life in schools: An introduction to critical pedagogy in the foundations of education* (4th edition). Boston: Allyn & Bacon.

Mc Neil, L. M. (2005). Creating new inequalities: Contradictions of reform. In H. S. Shapiro and D. E. Purpel (Eds.), *Ciritical social issues in American education: democracy and meaning in a globalizing world* (pp. 77–88). Mahwah, NJ: Lawrence Erlbaum Associates.

Morgan, A. (2006). Developing geographical wisdom: Post-formal thinking about, and relating to, the world. *International Research in Geographical & Environmental Education, 15*(4), 336–352.

Noblit, G. (1993). Power and caring. *American Educational Research Quarterly, 30*(1), 23–38.

Noddings, N. (2001). The care tradition: Beyond "Add women and stir." *Theory Into Practice, 40*(1), 29–34.

Noddings, N. (2005). Care and moral education. In H. S. Shapiro & D. E. Purpel (Eds.), *Critical social issues in American education: Democracy and meaning in a globalizing world* (3rd ed., pp. 297–308). Mahwah, NJ: Lawrence Erlbaum Associates, Inc.

Olssen, M. (2003). Structuralism, post-structuralism, neo-liberalism: assessing Foucault's legacy. *Journal of Educational Policy 18*(2), 189–202.

Peters, M. (2003). Post-structuralism and Marxism: education as knowledge capitalism. *Journal of Educational Policy 18*(3), 115–129.

Pitt, A. (2001). The dreamwork of autobiography: Felman, Freud, and Lacan. In Kathleen Weiler (Ed.), *Feminist engagements* (pp. 89–108. New York: Routledge.

Portes, A. (2005). English-only triumphs, but the costs are high. In H. S. Shapiro & D. E. Purpel (Eds.), *Critical social issues in American education: Democracy and meaning in a globalizing world.*

Rabaté, J. M. (Ed.) (2000). *Lacan in America*. New York: Other Press.

Rabaté, J. M. (2003). Lacan's return to Freud. In J. M. Rabaté (Ed.), *The Cambridge companion to Lacan* (pp. 1–24). Cambridge: Cambridge University Press.

Rabinovich, D. (2003). What is a Lacanian Clinic? In J. M. Rabaté (Ed.), *The Cambridge companion to Lacan* (pp. 208–220). Cambridge: Cambridge University Press.

Ragland, E. (1999). *Critical essays on Jacques Lacan.* New York: G.K. Hall.

Roudinesco, E. (2003). The mirror stage: An obliterated archive. In J. M. Rabaté (Ed.), *The Cambridge companion to Lacan* (pp. 25–34). Cambridge: Cambridge University Press.

Sadovnik A. R., Cookson, P. W., & Semel, S. F. (2001). *Exploring education: An introduction to the foundations of education* (2nd edition). Boston: Allyn & Bacon.

Shapiro, H. S. & Purpel, D. E. (Eds.) (2005). *Critical social issues in American Education: Democracy and meaning in a globalizing world.* Mahwah, NJ: Lawrence Erlmbaum Associates Publishers.

Shepherdson, C. (2003). Lacan and philosophy. In J. M. Rabaté (Ed.), *The Cambridge companion to Lacan* (pp. 116–152). Cambridge: Cambridge University Press.

Soslau, E. G. & Yost, D. S. (2007). Urban service-learning: An authentic teaching strategy to deliver a standards-driven curriculum. *Journal of Experiential Education 30*(1), 36–53.

Spillers, H. (1996). 'All the things you could be by now, if Sigmund Freud's wife was your mother: Psychoanalysis and race. *Boundary 2 23*(3), 75–140.

Spring, J. (2006). *American education* (12th edition). Boston: McGraw Hill.

Tatum, B. D. (1997). *Why are all the black kids sitting together in the cafeteria?: And other conversations about race*. New York: Perseus Books.

Thomas, D. (1993). Burke, Nietzsche, Lacan: Three perspectives on the rhetoric of order. *Quarterly Journal of Speech, 79*, 336–355.

West, C. (1999). *The Cornel West reader.* New York: Basic Civitas Books.

Zĭzek, S. (1991). *Looking awry: An introduction to Jacques Lacan through popular culture*. Cambridge, MA: The MIT Press.

Zĭzek, S. (2005). *Interrogating the real.* London: Continuum.

www.ingramcontent.com/pod-product-compliance
Lightning Source LLC
Chambersburg PA
CBHW071353230926
51846CB00002B/534